IS THAT A WORD?

DAVID BUKSZPAN

Is That a Word?

From AA to ZZZ, the Weird and Wonderful Language of SCRABBLE®

CHRONICLE BOOKS
SAN FRANCISCO

Library of Congress Cataloging-in-Publication Data is available.

ISBN: 978-1-4521-0824-7

Manufactured in China

Designed by Neil Egan
Typesetting by DC Type
Illustrations by David Hopkins

10 9 8 7 6 5 4 3 2 1

Chronicle Books LLC
680 Second Street
San Francisco, California 94107
www.chroniclebooks.com

CONTENTS

DISCLAIMER

This collection of words, tips, and history related to anagram crossword games, specifically Scrabble but also including Words With Friends, Lexulous, Bananagrams, and Snatch-It Word Game, is not sponsored by, endorsed by, written for, or approved by Hasbro, Inc., Zynga Inc., Bananagrams Inc., U.S. Games Systems, Inc., or any other game producer. In the text that follows, for ease of usage, simplified versions of game titles are used. By using the word "Scrabble," we mean "SCRABBLE® Brand Crossword Game." Scrabble is the trademark of Hasbro, Inc. in North America and Mattel in other countries around the world. By using the words "Words With Friends," we mean "Words With Friends®." Words With Friends is the trademark of Zynga Inc. By using the word "Lexulous," we mean "Lexulous®." Lexulous is the trademark of RJ Softwares. By using the word "Bananagrams," we mean "Bananagrams®." Bananagrams is a registered trademark of Bananagrams Inc. By using the words "Snatch-It" we mean "Snatch-It Word Game," which is produced by U.S. Game Systems, Inc.

ACKNOWLEDGMENTS

Hearty thank yous to Stephen Fatsis and Paul McCarthy, both of whose fine books on Scrabble were instrumental to the reporting in the first third of this volume. My gratitude also to my family, friends, and editor for your support and tolerance as I subjected you all to far too much jetsam of Scrabble minutia for far too long a time. And cheers to you, Alfred Mosher Butts; you created a helluva game.

INTRODUCTION

T HIS BOOK STARTED, quite literally, with a challenge. A few years back, a friend invited me to join her one warm spring day in Brooklyn's lovely Prospect Park for a game of Scrabble. I'm sure that, knowing full well my weaknesses for games, parks, and any excuse for an al fresco glass of wine, she wasn't surprised at how fast I arrived with a blanket, a board, and a box of sauvignon blanc. I hadn't played Scrabble in many years, but I had always been decent at the game and looked forward to showing off my skills. Oh, does nothing go as well rewarded in this world as overconfidence?

A couple of turns in, my friend played *za*. "Za?" I asked, "I don't think so," the incredulity in my voice leaving no room for my friend to do anything other than pick up her tiles and say she was kidding. "Yeah," she said, "za. Pizza. Like 'a slice of za.'" My eyes rolled and I couldn't help but feel a twang of sympathy, knowing full well that though a smart girl, my friend's large vocabulary of unusual slang terms was of no help in Scrabble. "I've got the dictionary right here," she offered. Confidently I flipped to the last page and backtracked a few pages to the spot under the giant Z tile marking the beginning of the letter's entries, expecting maybe a few words before **zag**. And I was right: there were a few words before **zag**. But the first of them was **za**.

I certainly didn't remember that word from my days growing up playing Scrabble. My friend scored her 20-odd points, and we continued. I was holding on to a slight lead. What I wasn't ready for was her play of **qi**—in two directions!—off a Triple Word Score that she'd opened up two turns later.

"Qi?" I asked, only slightly less skeptical than I'd been about za. "It's a type of Chinese eternal life force," she said flatly. Again she handed me the dictionary. This time she racked up 64 points, jumping out to a sizable lead. By the end of the game, it was all I could do to cover my annoyance, congratulate her on her victory, and not mutter these bizarre two-letter words to myself as I finished off the box of wine. It was a particular brand of annoyance, a kind of childish sour-grapes complaint that tried to dismiss her knowledge as a kind of cheating. I'd rather lose than have to try that hard, I thought, as I dropped into a local bookstore on my way home and picked up a copy of the newest edition of the Scrabble dictionary.

I did a little online research, and my friend and I continued to play as spring turned to summer. I started playing other friends, coworkers, and family members. I started playing strangers online. Some opponents knew some of these mystical, magical words that were capable of scoring huge amounts of points; others didn't. I kept playing and learning, and before long I found myself persuing the game section of my bookstore for books specifically about Scrabble.

I started with Stefan Fatsis's bestseller *Word Freak*, one of two of the best books ever written on Scrabble. The other is Paul McCarthy's *Letterati*. They are both fascinating, superbly researched insider's guides to the world of competitive Scrabble—the players, the tournaments, the gossip, and the history of the game. What they aren't, however, are books particularly suited to improving one's game. And suddenly that's what I was looking for more than anything else: a guide for a noncompetitive (the parlance is "parlor") player that was something different than mindnumbing lists of words found in so-called "players' guides." That's what I was after.

In reading *Word Freak* and *Letterati*, while I loved being let in to the world of competitive Scrabble (a world I knew from the start I never wanted to enter into), I also grew increasingly saddened. Saddened to learn that while the elite players—the contenders for the national and world championships—have utterly unbelievable numbers of unusual words memorized, they don't know (and don't seem to even care!) what a lot of those words mean.

This makes sense, of course. There's only so much capacity in the human mind. If the mission is to know as many words as possible, why waste cranial real estate with a bunch of definitions? A nice little bungalow housing seven-letter words containing two *c*s and two *e*s could be built there.

Yet here it is, a game unlike chess or backgammon, poker or dominos, that has the ability to transcend the 225 squares of its board—that offers the chance to take what's learned ostensibly to beat one's opponent and also use it to spruce up the conversation that night at dinner. On one side, we have players who know all the words and don't care about their definitions. On the other, players who maybe know some of these words, but who naturally somewhat resent people who memorize a lot of them. I started to feel there must be more people like me—folks who would like the game even more for its capacity to increase one's vocabulary. (Of course, this is nothing new. One of the most exciting aspects of Scrabble for its inventor was just that.) And thus this book, which indulges in some of my favorite aspects of my favorite game: its peculiar history and numerous iterations, helpful strategies, quirky facts, and, above all, its wonderful, wonderful words.

Scrabblish as a Second Language

The Scrabble lexicon, the game's authorized list of playable words for home use, is contained in the *Official Scrabble Players Dictionary*, often referred to as the *OSPD*. In its fourth edition, the paperback version is inexpensive but impressively comprehensive despite its small size, which has also helped make the *OSPD* the primary reference for settling disputes for all kinds of anagram-based games, from Bananagrams to Boggle. There's no rule that parlor players must use the *OSPD* for Scrabble, but for the sake of consistency and standardization, it's the logical choice. While not all online Scrabble-type games use the *OSPD,* those that do not tend to use lexicons that are very similar. Ultimately, if an industry standard other than the *OSPD* is taken up, it's hard to imagine that one will be chosen that risks alienating the many, many players who currently refer to the *OSPD* as their word-game bible.

Occasionally, when I play Scrabble against someone unacquainted with the Scrabble lexicon and I use a word not typically part of an average (or even above average) English speaker's vocabulary, the response is less one of curiosity than criticism. "See," an opponent is likely to say, "that's what I don't like about Scrabble: all those ridiculous words."

This book culls from the *OSPD* some of those ridiculous words, words that I personally find interesting for their definitions or linguistic construction and/or strategically helpful, with the hope not so much of making them any less odd or outlandish, but of embracing them for those reasons.

These words, while included in the *OSPD* because they're included in at least one of five other, standardized English dictionaries (more on this in History of the Scrabble Lexicon on page 38), often do not resemble the English language we know. The *OSPD* includes words like **teiid** and **xyst**, **cwm** and **kvas**, **ecu** and **fremd**. Even some of the words we might recognize, like **candle** or **necklace**, turn out to have meanings most English speakers would never imagine, opening up constructions as verbs like **candled** or **necklacing**.

In some ways, this book is less about Scrabble (and similar anagram games) than about the strange language that these games—most notably Scrabble—have given rise to, a language I like to think of as Scrabblish.

While it is a subset of English, Scrabblish consists of a wide array of words, many of which exist outside of most English speakers' vocabulary. As they're all legal ("playable") words in Scrabble, the Scrabblish lexicon contains no words that require capitalization or hyphenation. Often these words are archaic or obscure. In Scrabblish, an aged person who ate a piece of okra in the afternoon can also be described as an **oldster wha et ae bendy**.

Because even competitive Scrabble players with the greatest knowledge of the Scrabblish lexicon know but a fraction of the definitions of these words, I feel safe in saying that Scrabblish, while studied meticulously, is still unspoken—and for that we should be thankful. Still, I find Scrabblish utterly charming (and quite literally very playful), as well as a fascinating gateway into the possibilities that the English language offers, if we only care to look.

How Words Are Designated

This book categorizes words into three sets: words (like **chair**) that are playable in Scrabble and included in the *OSPD* for parlor play, words (like ***shit***) that are playable in Scrabble tournaments but are censored from or too long to be included in the *OSPD* (more on this difference in The History of the Scrabble Lexicon, pg. 38), and words (like <u>Santa</u>) that are not allowed in Scrabble. Words from the first set are in **bold**, words from the second set are in ***bold and italics***, and words from the last group are <u>underlined</u>.

Definitions are almost always based on the ones offered in the *OSPD*, which favors uncommon usages, but occasionally the more common usage is invoked. Words are almost always used in the part of speech given/favored by the *OSPD* to highlight possible suffixes.

Some Scrabblish alternatives to common words are sprinkled throughout the text in this book. Definitions are located in nearby sidebars for convenience.

Ways to Improve Your Game

While learning some of the words in this book should improve your Scrabble game substantially, its purpose is not solely to make you a better player. There's some of that, to be sure, but if you really want to improve your game, there are other options available to you. Namely: play a lot, especially against much better players (online games or matches against a computer program work fine); buy any or all of the wonderful, exhaustive players' guidebooks that exist; or simply pick up a copy of the *OSPD*, study it, create flash cards and lists, and slowly kiss that pesky social life of yours good-bye.

This book is first and foremost about having fun with the words and the game. Scrabble set, park, and box of wine sold separately.

PART 1

The Story of Scrabble and Beyond:
The Game's Creation, Mutations, and Relations, Plus a Look at Its Most Remarkable Records

Scrabble was born in Queens, came of age in downtown New York chess clubs, and has been entertaining and challenging players ever since. But that's not to say it hasn't experienced its growing pains along the way. As the game has evolved, so have its spinoffs and various online iterations—and so has Scrabble's official dictionary, which came under fire for some of its more noxious entries. Finally, no study of the game would be complete without a moment to celebrate some of its players' most fantastic feats, from winning with negative points to what might be the greatest Scrabble play ever.

Alfred Mosher Butts
Recession Is the Mother of Invention

It was the 1930s, and an out-of-work, thirty-three-year-old architect with diverse interests and an obsessive personality thought Americans could use a new game to help pass the hard times. Working out of his fifth-floor walk-up in the Queens, New York, neighborhood of Jackson Heights, Alfred Mosher Butts started by writing a three-page "History of Games" in which he made three classifications: "men-on-a-board games" like chess and backgammon, numbers games using dice or cards, and games involving letters and words. Butts was particularly fond of backgammon, which he thought correctly balanced the elements of skill and luck to create "a much more satisfactory and enduring amusement." Studying the overall landscape of the games industry in the United States, Butts determined that the category that showed the most promise for innovation was word games, of which the prevailing model at the time was a game called Anagrams.

Anagrams is reputed to date back to Victorian England, and it is still one of the most popular non-Scrabble games among Scrabble tournament players. Selchow & Righter, the first established game company to produce Scrabble, was already producing a game called Anagrams when it bought the rights to Scrabble. Anagrams involved players overturning tiles, evenly distributed across the alphabet, one at a time to create words. (Today, Anagrams is most often played with Scrabble tiles, but it is also available for purchase as a game called Snatch It.)

Butts's breakthrough in improving Anagrams came when he read Edgar Allan Poe's "The Gold Bug," in which a character tries to crack a code of symbols to find a hidden treasure. The code is solved by

Alfredo: an Italian sauce of cream, butter, cheese, and garlic

Mosher: one who dances violently to rock music

Butt: to strike with a thrust of the head

comparing the frequency of certain symbols with their frequency in the English language, starting with that most recurrent of letters, *e*. Butts realized that a game that took into account the proportion of different letters in English words, instead of simply producing an equal number of each letter (akin to playing cards), would make game play easier, yet still incorporate a strong factor of the luck of the draw.

And so Butts launched into the creation of Lexiko, the first iteration of Scrabble. It's often said that Butts created the letter distribution by dissecting the front page of the *New York Times*; actually he used pages from the *Times*, the *New York Herald Tribune*, and the *Saturday Evening Post*. Butts sold the first copies of Lexiko in 1933.

Butts continued to **tew** at the game, adding a board, adding premium squares, reworking the distribution and number of tiles, tweaking the rules. He tested Lexiko at home with his **feme**, manufactured sets in his living room, and sold them by word of mouth: by August 1934, he'd sold eighty-four sets at about $1.50 a game **fer** $127. But he'd had to **wair** $147 on plywood, ink, glue, and such. The game grew in popularity so that Butts had to **moil** to keep up with Christmas orders, but when he tried selling the game to a large **biz**, Milton Bradley, Parker Brothers, and the publishing house Simon and Schuster all passed. In 1938, he changed the name of the game from Lexiko to Criss-Cross Words.

Butts eventually gave up his search for a buyer, but in 1947 a lawyer made him an offer and bought the rights; Butts would receive a small royalty. (Butts lived out his life collecting checks large enough to live comfortably, but far smaller than one might expect for creating a game that would become—and remain—so incredibly popular.) The lawyer tinkered with the board, farmed out much of the production, and changed the name to Scrabble. The name was chosen in small part for its meaning (to grope about frantically), in large part for its

Tew: to work hard	**Wair:** to spend
Feme: a wife	**Moil:** to work
Fer: for	**Biz:** a business

The only anagram of **Scrabble** is **clabbers**: to beat badly.

evocation of the word *scramble*, and certainly not least because there was no similar trademarked name.

Sales continued to rise until 1952, when legend has it that Macy's chairman Jack Straus played Scrabble during his vacation on Long Island. He quickly became totally taken with it but was surprised to learn that his store didn't carry the game. He submitted a large order and other stores soon followed suit. By the end of the year, two thousand sets were being sold a week. A year later, the Queen of England was spotted buying a set in New York and sales so skyrocketed that the *Herald Tribune* wrote that 1953 could be memorable for "any number of notable events, from the inauguration of a Republican president to the growth of Scrabble."

Nearly four million sets were sold in 1954, and sales have remained strong ever since, as the American rights were first sold to Selchow & Righter, then transferred to Coleco, and most recent to Hasbro. It's estimated that worldwide sales are still around three or four million sets per year, with the recent increase in the popularity of online play creating a fresh surge in traditional sets. Scrabble has now sold more than 150 million sets worldwide and can be found in a third of American homes.

From *Life* magazine, December 14, 1953

"Christmas shoppers in search of the standard $2 Scrabble set can get it in only two ways: they can place their names on the bottom of waiting lists, or they can lurk for hours beside a counter until a shipment arrives, at which time they take their chances like football players going after a fumble. No game in the history of the trade has ever sold so rapidly and few have shown such promise of consistent, long term popularity."

The Letter of the Law
Clarifying Certain Rules

One of the beautiful aspects of Scrabble is the relative simplicity of its rules and game play. Even so, some procedural questions occasionally crop up that are unaddressed in the short rule book packaged with each set. While players are welcome to follow their own house rules, here is a rundown of the rules of the finer points of the game as they have been agreed upon for competitive play in the United States, offered here primarily in the hope of helping maintain the domestic peace.

STARTING THE GAME

Players begin by drawing one tile each. The player with a tile closest to the beginning of the alphabet goes first. A blank supersedes an A. If two or more players tie, only the tied players draw again. Once the order is established, players return their tiles to the bag, and the player to go first picks his letters first. Play proceeds clockwise.

ENDING THE GAME

The game ends when no tiles remain in the bag and one player has played all his tiles, or when all players pass three times consecutively. In two-player Scrabble, the player who finishes all his tiles first receives twice the value of his opponent's tiles. In games of more than two players, the player who finishes first receives the sum of all the opponents' tiles, and each opponent subtracts the sum of the tiles on his own rack from his own score. If play ends without any player using all his tiles, the sum of each player's rack is subtracted from his score. Blanks have no value. High score wins. Ties exist—there is no tiebreaker. (In tournaments, a tie counts as half a win and half a loss.)

SCORING PREMIUM SQUARES AND THE BINGO BONUS

Double or Triple Letter Scores are computed in a play's score before a Double or Triple Word Score. A 50-point bonus for a "bingo" (using all seven letters in one play) is added on only after any multiplication has taken place.

National Scrabble Day

National Scrabble Day is celebrated each year on April 13, and it commemorates Alfred Mosher Butts's birthday in 1899. Generally, the Scrabble-obsessed celebrate by indulging in their obsession, but one might also consider observing the day by speaking Scrabblish, or at least peppering one's speech with *q*-without-*u* words.

DRAWING TILES

Tiles should be kept in an opaque bag. When a player draws tiles, the player's eyes should be averted and the bag should be held at arm's length and eye level. Feeling the face of a tile with one's fingers to discern what it is (known as "**brailling**") is not allowed.

In Scrabble parlance, to **braille** is to cheat by feeling the face of a letter when it's in the bag. Games in Scrabble tournaments are played with flat-faced plastic letters called Protiles to eliminate brailling (sets of Protiles can be purchased online for about $20). The *Official Scrabble Players Dictionary* defines braille as "to write in braille," but there's also to **brail**, to haul in a sail—which offers a kind of double entendre to the Scrabble players' usage. Of course, all of this is moot for blind Scrabble players, for whom sets with braille tiles exist, which themselves must be terrifically simple to braille if tiles are chosen from a bag rather than by first being laid out facedown on the table.

DRAWING TOO MANY TILES AT ONCE

It sometimes happens that a player picks too many tiles during a turn, and doesn't notice that he has too many tiles until they are already on his rack. The player's opponent then gets to select as many tiles as have been overdrawn plus two additional tiles to look at, and then choose whichever tile(s) he wants to return to the bag to correct the guilty player's rack. If the extra tiles have not been integrated into the player's rack, the opponent chooses only from the newly chosen tiles.

TRADING IN TILES

A player can use a turn to trade in one to seven tiles at any time in the game until there are fewer than seven tiles left in the bag. The player should announce the number of tiles he's trading in, set those tiles face down to the side, then choose replacements, and only then return the tiles he's trading in to the bag. Of course, a player receives no points for that turn, but learning when it's wise to exchange tiles is a skill that's worth its weight in blanks.

Recycling Tiles: Ecological Scrabble

One slight rule change that can make classic Scrabble a bit more interesting and fun—not to mention a fair bit easier—is to allow players to replace the blank once it has been played. Sometimes this is called Ecological Scrabble, as the blank is "recycled." Under this adaptation, a blank played on the board in one turn can be substituted for the letter it represents by any player on a subsequent turn. The caveat is that the blank must be used at once by the player who picks it up. Another version allows players to replace the blank with any letter that would create a legal play. Points are awarded for any new word(s) created using the blank, but not for the word(s) created by replacing the blank with a letter.

THE CHALLENGE RULE

In competitive Scrabble, there's no rule that says one must play a legal word. But if a word is challenged and is found not to be legal (called a **phony** in Scrabble parlance), the player who set it down loses his turn. Conversely, if a challenged word is found to be playable, the challenger loses his turn. When a play is challenged, all new words that may have been made during a turn are included in the challenge, and

Challenging Evolution

In the early days of competitive Scrabble, the standard "look-up rule" dictated that the player who played the word had to look up the word if challenged. Today this seems odd, as it gives the player a chance to find other possible plays for the next turn if the challenged word is not listed. But at the time, the de facto dictionary for play was the *Funk & Wagnalls College Dictionary*, and words in it were often hard to find (one had to know that **maria** was the plural of **mare**, and so would be found under **mare**, for example). So the onus was on the player to know the dictionary well. Having an opponent look up a word could punish a player if the opponent didn't know where to find it. Today in competitive play, it's standard to have an impartial party do the adjudicating.

the invalidity of any of them results in the loss of the entire turn. It's a system that rewards knowledge (and confidence in one's knowledge) of the official word list.

Basic Strategizing

Despite their stated point values, some tiles are worth more than others. Anyone who's ever played Scrabble knows good letters (the blank, S, R, X, etc.) from bad tiles (the V and C don't form any two-letter words, so they can be particularly annoying). The trick is not to waste good letters for small scores and to unload bad letters (by playing them or trading them in) without letting them sit on your rack too long and ruin the chance for a bingo, or at least for drawing better letters.

ESSES TO EXCESS

They say you can't have too much of a good thing, so it might follow that the more Ss in your rack, the better. But as having two Ss at once actually decreases the chances of scoring a bingo, if you're holding more than one, it's often best to play off the extras as soon as possible and hold on to a single S until the timing for a big play is right.

KEEP TRACK OF THE POWER TILES, BLANKS, AND SS

Particularly as the game progresses, it's helpful to know what tiles your opponent might be holding. This is nowhere near as hard as counting cards—and it's perfectly legal. Scrabble boards even have the tile distribution numbers printed on them off to the side.

The main tiles to keep track of are the "power tiles," the five highest-scoring tiles, of which there is only one apiece: Z, Q, X, J, and K. Before you play an A right below a Triple Letter Score, check to see if your opponent might have the Z. It could be a 60-plus point difference. Know the two-letter words using these tiles, and be mindful of them even when you don't have these letters. And certainly, knowing how many blanks or Ss are out there can inform a decision about whether to make a certain play.

Dynamic Duos: The Ten Most Important (i.e., highest-scoring) Two-Letter Words

Do not turn the page until your learn this list.

Za: pizza

Qi: the central life force in traditional Chinese culture, pronounced as "chee" (also **ki**)

Jo: a sweetheart

Ax: a tool for chopping wood

Ex: to cross something out

Ox: a large mammal (pl. -en) or a large, oafish person (pl. -es)

Xi: a Greek letter (*pronounced like the zai in* bonsai)

Xu: a monetary unit of Vietnam equal to one-hundredth of a **dong** (*derived from the French* **sou**) (also **sau**)

Ka: the eternal soul in ancient Egyptian spirituality

Ki: the life force in traditional Chinese culture, pronounced as "chee" (also **qi**)

Variations on a Theme
Non-Scrabble Word Games

GAMES BY HASBRO

Over the years, Hasbro and previous owners of the Scrabble brand have released a number of spin-off games bearing the Scrabble name and alternative anagram word games. Of the bunch, UpWords and Super Scrabble have proven the most popular, but there are plenty of others currently available in stores, or on offer at yard sales.

UpWords: An excellent "three-dimensional" Scrabble-like game that can sometimes be even **funner** than Scrabble, UpWords is played with stackable tiles, creating the opportunity to change letters in words as well as build off them. For instance, an F tile can be played atop the B in **boxes** to create **foxes**, and then used perpendicularly to make **flap**. UpWords is a faster game than Scrabble, and in a way more aesthetically pleasing: what better treat for the lover of words than to watch as a little three-dimensional city of various-sized towers built of letters springs up over the course of a game?

Super Scrabble: A much larger board with more than twice as many tiles plus quadruple premium squares combine to make this super-sized Scrabble game higher scoring. With its 21-by-21-square board, one can nerd out like never before and finally play *pseudosophistications*!

Scrabble Slam: A card game in which players rush to place cards in the center to form words. A low-stakes way to bone up on four-letter words—especially when playing against opponents with larger **vocabs** (vocabularies). It moves fast but gets old fast, too.

Scrabble Scramble: In this decent on-the-go Scrabble spin-off, players shake out dice with letters on each face and make words on a tiny Scrabble board. A good way to pass half an hour at the beach with your librarian friend, it's a slightly improved version of the old Crosswords game by Milton Bradley.

Scrabble Upper Hand: Billed as a "grand slam word game," this mix of Scrabble and Bridge (why it wasn't simply called Scribbidge I can't understand) came out from Selchow and Righter. It didn't last long. This game is not to be confused with the still extant Kings Cribbage (put out by Conoco, not Hasbro) which is basically Cribbage played on a Scrabble board. It's not terribly easy to pick up, and seems destined to remain forever abandoned and gathering dust in the great toy attic of history.

Scrabble Overturn: Overturn was an interesting "spin" on Scrabble, incorporating aspects of Othello (Go). Each tile is a cylinder with the same letter printed on it four times in four different colors. Each player (up to four) is assigned a color, and as a word is played on the board, the player turns all the tiles in that word to her color, as well as tiles in any other accompanying new words. For instance, if **zag** is on the board in green, and the player using purple letters creates **zags** and **sugar**, all the letters in **sugar**, plus the former **zag** (as it's now **zags**) are turned to purple. Players record scores for words created as the game progresses, and these are added to points totaled at the end of the game for the words that are then in each player's color. Unfortunately, the round tiles are difficult to manipulate in the racks, and if one is dropped it has a habit of rolling away. Still, this is a good game to pick up at a yard sale (it's been out of print for years); just don't play it on the top of a hill.

BOLDLY PLAYING: STAR TREK SCRABBLE

Scrabble is in many ways the *Law & Order* of board games: it's cheap to produce, very addictive, and there have been far too many spin-offs to count. And though there hasn't yet been a *Law & Order* Scrabble spin-off (wouldn't <u>mccoy</u> make a great word?), it probably wouldn't be the oddest. Spin-off sets based on such franchises as *Shrek, The Wizard of Oz, Major League Baseball,* the Chicago Cubs (perhaps a good gift to give an adversary, as the Cubs haven't won a championship in over a century), the New York Yankees (<u>yankee</u> isn't playable but **yanqui**, meaning an American citizen, is), *The Simpsons, Dora the Explorer,* John Deere, and *Star Trek* have all been unleashed. Beyond their thematically stylized boards, the spin-offs include allowances for the lexical idiosyncrasies of their subjects, including bonus points for certain words.

The *Star Trek* edition, for instance, offers bonus points for **captain** and <u>vulcan</u>, which is legal in that game only. Triple Word Scores are

called <u>Tribble</u> Word Scores. Even the very language of the game play is altered: when exchanging tiles, players are instructed to announce, "I am a doctor, not a linguist!" and when a challenge is called for, the challenger is to suggest that the word seems "illogical."

Howbeit (nevertheless), you don't need a special *Star Trek* set to play *Star Trek*–like words, nor do you need to know <u>Klingon</u> (although when you see the words that champion tournament players make, it often looks like they do). While <u>Spock</u> isn't good, there are some words that are playable in a traditional Scrabble game that may resemble the Trekkie words you're familiar with.

<u>Scotty</u> is no good in Scrabble, but you can bring your **scottie** to the game. You can even dress him in a **sulu** and watch him play behind the **kirk**. <u>Whoopi Goldberg</u> can't come either, but a **whoopie** can cheer you on. Choose your opponent wisely: beware the wrath of a **khan**. If you beat him, soothe his anger with a bouquet of **phlox**. (In case you were wondering, the species known as volcano phlox is not **vulcanic**.)

Scottie: a type of terrier

Sulu: a Malaysian skirt

Kirk: a church

Whoopie: one who cheers loudly (also **whoopee**)

Khan: an Asian ruler

Phlox: a genus of flowering plants

Vulcanic: pertaining to volcanoes

PRESIDENTIAL SCRABBLE

Barack Obama is a self-described Scrabble fan, George W. Bush has said his favorite iPad **app** is Scrabble, and Bill Clinton passed much of his time after his heart surgery playing UpWords. But for those who want a hefty serving of presidential politics infused into their crossword board game, Presidential Scrabble is also available. Like other Scrabble spin-offs, Presidential Scrabble changes the board a little (it's round instead of square and offers bonus squares based on the Electoral College votes of different states), awards extra points for using some themed lingo (like **vote**), adds to the playable lexicon (LBJ and FDR are good), and otherwise toys with the original (a deck of cards featuring presidents offers special privileges—the Nixon card allows a player to be pardoned for misspelling a word).

But there was already plenty of presidential stuff in the regular old, plain-**jane** (Adams) version of Scrabble. For instance, the names of many **prezes** are also common nouns and are thus playable: **Pierce, Grant, Hoover, Ford, Carter,** and **Bush.** President (and former **veep**) *Johnson* is only invited to participate in tournament play.

Bush: to cover with shrubs

Carter: one who carts

Clintonia: an herb of the lily family with yellow, white, or purple flowers

Ford: to cross

Grant: to permit

Hoover: to use a vacuum cleaner

Johnson: a penis

Pierce: to puncture

Prex: a president, usually of a college (also **prexy**)

Prez: a president

Veep: vice president

OTHER SCRABBLE-LIKE GAMES

The Scrabble lexicon isn't the only part of the game that allows for seemingly endless variation; there are lots of ways to tinker with the game itself. Online and mobile games have exploded in popularity in recent years, as have more analog and less traditional versions of the classic anagrams game.

Trickster Less Tricky

In 2010, Mattel, which owns the rights to Scrabble everywhere except in North America, debuted Scrabble Trickster. Scrabble Trickster is not available in North America, and is basically classic Scrabble, except that it permits proper nouns, and if words are placed on particular tiles, players may spell words backward or "steal" tiles from other players. The game's release garnered a lot of attention on both sides of the pond, much of which was critical of its apparent aim to court players with pop culture at the expense of building and rewarding vocabulary skills. Articles lambasted Trickster for allowing names like JayZ, Lady Gaga, and Barack Obama. But while one cannot play proper nouns as such in classic Scrabble, the original does allow for **Jay**, **Zee**, **Lady**, **Gaga**, **Barrack** (careful, two Rs here), **Oba**, and **Ma**.

Jay: the letter *j*

Zee: the letter *z*

Shawn: a past tense of shaw

Carter: one who carts

Lady: a woman

Gaga: insane

Barrack: to shout

boisterously

Oba: a hereditary chief in Benin and Nigeria

Ma: mother

SPEED SCRABBLE/BANANAGRAMS

As the name suggests, Speed Scrabble is a fast, less formal variant of Scrabble. Also known as "Take Two" (with slightly different rules) and similar to Bananagrams, Speed Scrabble is played with Scrabble tiles but without the board.

Bananagrams is a product completely independent of Scrabble, consisting of 144 tiles (as opposed to Scrabble's 100 tiles) without point values in a **cavendish**-esque purse (made of yellow cloth, not **abaca**). Its rules vary slightly from Speed Scrabble, but it is essentially the same game. Perhaps the most noticeable difference is the banana-centric lingo used in the game, like saying "Split" to begin the game and "Peel" to pick another tile.

RULES

1. All the tiles are set **facedown** in the center of a playing space **atween** the players.
2. Each player draws seven tiles and at the word "Go" flips the tiles

and commences to make her own crossword configuration of the letters.

3. As soon as one player uses all seven of her tiles, she announces, "Pick one!" and each player picks an additional tile from the upside-down tiles in the center. (A popular form of this game has players pick two tiles at a time.) Each player continues to reconfigure her own crossword in the attempt to incorporate all her own tiles.

4. Play continues with a player announcing "Pick one!" as soon as she has incorporated all her tiles into her crossword.

5. The round ends when there are not enough tiles for all players to pick a tile (or two tiles) each, and then the first player to incorporate all her tiles into her crossword wins.

6. The winner is awarded the total point value of all other players' unused tiles, and each other player subtracts the total of her own unused tiles from her own score.

7. All words in the *OSPD* are legal, though **vulgo** (often) it's **mair** (more) fun and challenging to play without two-letter words. (Familiarity with the words in this book is particularly useful in Speed Scrabble.)

8. Often, a bonus of 10 points is awarded to players for each seven-letter (or longer) word they have created, or for the longest word of the round.

Cavendish: a process of curing tobacco (*When referring to the Cavendish banana, it's capitalized.*)

Abaca: a species of banana harvested for its hemp (also **abaka**)

Facedown: with the face-side downward

Atween: between

Vulgo: often

Mair: more

WARNINGS AND TIPS

1. It's usually beneficial to try to create long words, as they'll create more hooks for additional words.

2. Don't neglect to inspect the winner's crossword—often there are

tiles from an old word that were not moved as the player changed her board. And make sure she hasn't conveniently played an upside-down M as a W somewhere.

Note: Speed Scrabble is also the name of a form of traditional Scrabble played extremely quickly, similar to Speed Chess. While competitive Scrabble is generally played with a time limit of 25 minutes per player, Speed Scrabble allots only three minutes per competitor. A point is deducted for every second taken over the three-minute limit. The engaging Scrabble documentary *Word Wars*, based on Stephen Fatsis's book, *Word Freak*, contains footage of one such match, and it's pretty impressive.

ANAGRAMS

Anagrams, also known as the board game Snatch-It, is probably the most common Scrabble variant played by competitive Scrabble players. Like Speed Scrabble, it's fast moving and played without a board. But it reveals itself as a more cutthroat contest in that all players have access to tiles as soon as they're turned over, and players can steal ("snatch") each other's tiles after opponents have already incorporated them into words.

RULES

1. Play starts with all the tiles facedown between all competitors. Players establish rules beforehand governing the minimum length of playable words and whether adding simple prefixes like *re-* and *un-* and suffixes like *-er*, *-ed*, and *-ing* are legal.
2. Players take turns turning over one tile at a time, leaving the overturned tiles in the center of the playing space.
3. When a player sees a word that can be made from the overturned tiles, she announces the word and takes the tiles, forming the word in front of her so the other players can see it.
4. As tiles continue to be turned over, players can use any combination of tiles in the center or other players' complete words (called stealing) to create new words (a player may use an S with an opponent's **rate** to create **stare**, for instance). The new word is placed in front of the player who makes it.

5. Play ends when all the tiles are overturned and no player can make a new word.

6. If two players call out different words at the same time, the longer word takes precedence. If words are of the same length, the higher scoring (based on the tiles' points) takes precedence. If point totals are also the same, or the same word is called out by two players simultaneously, players draw letters, and the closest to the beginning of the alphabet takes precedence. Letters overturned for this reason are then flipped over again and mixed back in with the remaining tiles.

7. Scoring can be determined by the number of tiles, words, or points of the tiles each player has in front of him. Bonus points for words of a certain length may also be awarded.

WARNINGS AND TIPS

1. It's often best to play with two sets of Scrabble tiles at once, offering longer game play and thus more possibilities to create anagrams of longer words.

2. If playing with children, consider allowing them to create shorter words. (Then steal their words from them—tough love breeds champions!)

PLAY WITH T AND A: STRIP SCRABBLE

Perhaps the most **risque** permutation of Scrabble around is Strip Scrabble. No matter how cold your letters are, play can turn steamy at any moment. And it's the only version of the game that encourages competitors to show each other their racks. What's not to love?

RULES

1. In this game in particular, it's important to set the ground rules early: players should agree at the outset to wear the same number of articles of clothing; how much **nakeder** everyone feels comfortable becoming (maybe you want to stop at your **undies**), and what exactly constitutes an article of clothing (good rules of thumb: jewelry

Risque: verging on impropriety

Nakeder: more naked

Undies: underwear

Sox: plural of sock (also **socks**)

Aff: off

Moppet: a child

Cummer: a godmother

Granny: a grandmother

Aa: a type of stony, rough lava (pronounced a'ah) (*A Hawaiian word, it also originally meant "burn."*)

Bee: the letter *b*

Cee: the letter *c*

Dee: the letter *d*

Doubled: multiplied by two

Vino: wine

Vera: very

Oot: out

should not count and a pair of **sox** should be considered one article—the one sock on and one **aff** look doesn't do anybody any favors).

2. Play involves a normal Scrabble set and follows all the rules of Scrabble, with the following exceptions:
   - A player who scores less than 10 points (or 20 points, depending on the skills of the players) in a turn—including trading in tiles—must take off one article of clothing.
   - If a player makes use of a Triple Word Score, all other players take off an article of clothing.
   - If a player scores a bingo, all other players take off two articles of clothing.

3. At the end of the game, all players except the winner (though fair play might dictate the winner also) shed all remaining clothes to the agreed upon level of nudity. If everyone's already naked, the question must be asked: why are you still playing?

WARNINGS AND TIPS

1. Should not be played with **moppet**s, **cummers**, or **grannies**—especially my **granny**!

2. Use caution: tiles have a way of sticking to the skin (also: hiding tiles on one's person is generally frowned up—unless it's a really good hiding spot).

3. Unfortunately, xxx is not legal, even with an X and both blanks. **Aa** is the only playable bra size, unless one counts **bee**, **cee**, **dee**, and of course, **doubleD**.

Now I Know My A, Bee, Cees: Alphabets

The letter a is spelled, simply, "a"—so it's too short to be played in Scrabble, and the plural, <u>aes</u>, is also not playable. The same goes for e and its plural, <u>ees</u>, i and <u>ies</u>, and u and <u>ues</u>. As it and its plural are hyphenated, "<u>double-u</u>" is clearly not playable. However, **ae** is playable (adj., one), and **oes** makes it in as the plural of **oe** (a wind off the Faeroe islands).

The rest of the English alphabet is all fair game:

bee	**kay**	**es** and **ess**
cee	**el** and **ell**	**tee**
dee	**em**	**vee**
ef and **eff**	**en**	**ex**
gee	**pee**	**wye**
aitch	**kue**	**zee** and **zed** and **izzard**
jay	**ar**	

Other Alphabets

The names of the twenty-four Greek letters are all playable words.

Ere eta comes **zeta**, and **phi** is found **nigh chi**.

Ere: before

Nigh: near

Alpha	**Epsilon**	**Iota**
Beta	**Zeta**	**Kappa**
Gamma	**Eta**	**Lambda**
Delta	**Theta**	**Mu**

Nu	Rho	Phi
Xi	Sigma	Chi (also **khi**)
Omicron	Tau	Psi
Pi	Upsilon	Omega

The names of all the Hebrew letters are playable words.

Alef, aleph (**alif** is an Arabic letter)	Tet, teth	Fe, feh
Bes, beth	Yod, yodh	Pe, peh
Gimel	Kaf, kaph, khaf, khaph	Sade, sadhe, sadi, tsade, tsadi
Daledh, daleth	Lamed, lamedh	Koaph, qoph, caph
Heh	Mem	Resh
Vau, vav, vaw, waw	Nun	Sin
Zayin	Samech, samek, samekh	Shin
Cheth, het, heth, khet, kheth	Ain, ayin	Tav

4. Subsets of words—such as types of clothing, parts of the anatomy, or words having to do with sex—can be determined at the outset of the game to be wild cards and, when played, cause opponents to shed an article of clothing.

5. Contrary to its effect on most types of Scrabble games, booze (especially **vino**) **vera** much increases the level and enjoyment of play.

6. If everyone's wearing a lot of clothes because it's cold **oot**—or perhaps if your opponents are particularly hot—consider adding the caveat that at the end of each round, everyone but the player with the highest point total for that round takes off one article of clothing.

7. Team play is strongly encouraged.

HAGGLE SCRABBLE

There are two versions of Scrabble that incorporate money to make the game a little easier and a little more interesting. The first is Haggle Scrabble, the second is Cheaters' Scrabble. Games can be played using Monopoly money. The Monopoly amounts are given on the next page; if using cash, divide numbers by 100.

In Haggle Scrabble, sometimes known as Bartering Scrabble, players start without any money. Players' points are awarded as money at the end of each turn. So a player who makes a 26-point move is given $26. (No need for that pesky score sheet!) As players accumulate money, they can offer deals to their opponents. Players can make an offer to trade letters with opponents (the whole rack or a certain number of letters, either by first inspecting the opponent's rack or

Little Words, Big Money: Two- and Three-Letter Currency Words

It's obvious that short words, even if they themselves don't score a lot of points, are very valuable in Scrabble. They provide openings for longer words, as well as opportunities to position words on a board cramped with letters. But some small words are also valuable off the board: the English words for foreign currencies.

Xu and **zaire** are probably the most profitable, although **avo**, **ecu**, **jun**, **lek**, and **lev** also offer a lot of bang for the buck. I'm still hoping to play my favorite, **ngwee**, a monetary unit of Zambia that's worth one-hundredth of a **kwacha**. (At present, a ngwee is worth about 2 ten-thousandths of an American cent; I'd rather take the 9 points.)

Here's how to cash in:

Att: a unit of currency in Laos (pl. **att**)

Avo: a unit of currency in Macao

Ban: a unit of currency in Romania (pl. **bani**)

Ecu: a former French coin

Euro: a unified currency of much of Europe; also an Australian marsupial

Fil: a coin used in Iraq and Jordan

Hao: a unit of currency in Vietnam (pl. **hao**)

Jun: a coin used in North Korea (pl. **jun**)

Lek: a unit of currency in Albania (pl. -s, -e, or -u)

Leu: a unit of currency in Romania (pl. **lei**)

Lev: a unit of currency in Bulgaria (pl. **leva**)

Pul: a coin used in Afghanistan (pl. **puls** or **puli**)

Pya: a copper coin of Burma

Sen: a unit of currency in Japan

Som: a unit of currency in Kyrgyzstan

Sou: a former French coin

Zuz: an ancient Hebrew silver coin (pl. **zuzim**)

blindly swapping), to pay an opponent to pass his turn, to swap turns, or just about any other cheat they can think of. Players can also make offers to try to influence an opponent's move ("I'll give you $50 to open up a Triple Word Score for me"), to have a look at an opponent's rack, or even for advice. Whoever has the most money at the end of the game wins.

CHEATERS' SCRABBLE

In Cheaters' Scrabble, players start with $1,000 Monopoly money to spend as they will. Unlike in Haggle Scrabble, money is not awarded for points, and the winner is whoever has the most points at the end of the game. A New York City–based nonprofit that tutors students in creative writing, called 826nyc, held a Cheaters' Scrabble tournament. Their price list is a good model to use as a price guide:

- $500: Invent a Word—just pronounce it and define it, and it can't be challenged
- $250: Reject a Word—an opponent must remove his played word, redraw tiles, and lose his turn
- $200: Surf the 'Net—the chance to look up words on the Internet for two minutes
- $150: Add Q, X, or Z—add to any word and it counts

- $150: Buy a Vowel—trade a vowel from your rack for any tile you want in the bag
- $100: Add 10 to a Tile—add 10 points to a tile's value
- $100: Create a Blank—turn any tile in your rack over and make it a blank
- $100: Opponent's Rack—see an opponent's tiles
- $75: Name & Place—play a proper noun
- $50: Exchange a Tile—trade in a tile on your rack for a random tile without losing a turn
- $50: Passport—use a word from a foreign language

PLAYING ONLINE

SCRABULOUS/LEXULOUS

With the launch of an **online** platform in 2005, Scrabble began to experience a surge in popularity it hadn't seen since its earliest days. Except the online version wasn't exactly Scrabble; it was Scrabulous, a word game closely replicating the original. Created by two brothers in Kolkata, India, and originally available only through the Scrabulous **website**, the game exploded in 2007 when it became possible for **netops** to play one another via Facebook. Scrabulous duplicated Scrabble's board layout, letter values, tile distribution, and rules, and the creators were soon bringing in over $25,000 a month in **ad** revenue. But it was not to last: in 2008, Hasbro filed suit under the Digital Millennium Copyright Act, and five days later Facebook disabled the game for North American users. Within a month, Scrabulous was pulled in all other countries except India.

After a ruling in the Delhi High Court, Scrabulous was rereleased as Lexulous. Beyond the name, other dissimilarities to Scrabble were incorporated. The board layout was rearranged, tile distribution and point values were slightly altered, and players are dealt eight tiles at

Online: connected to a computer or telecommunications system

Website: one or more internally connected web pages accessible on the Internet

Ad: an advertisement

Ami: a friend (**Amie:** a female friend)

Cellphone: a wireless phone on a cellular network (also **cellular**)

Tablet: to write on a flat surface

Netop: a friend

Freeware: free software

App: a computer application

Netiquette: online etiquette

Kibitz: to chat informally (also **kibbitz**)

Befriend: to make a friend of

a time. These days Lexulous continues to flourish with more than $300,000 in revenue per year.

WORDS WITH **AMIS**: WORDS WITH FRIENDS

Words With Friends (WWF) was released in 2009 and has become another popular way to play a Scrabble-like game on *cellphones* and **tablets**, and one of the most popular cellphone **freeware apps** in general. Many games (currently up to twenty) can be played at once. Texans Paul and David Bittner created the game in 2009 and later sold it for more than $50 million. While it's considered bad etiquette to speak to one's opponent when face to face in a Scrabble tournament, it's not bad **netiquette** to **kibitz** with and even **befriend** strangers through Words With Friends.

To avoid the sorts of legal issues with Hasbro that Scrabulous encountered (and perhaps also to increase scoring possibilities), Words With Friends modifies some of the aspects of Scrabble while keeping many of the fundamental characteristics intact. While Scrabble purists may dislike straying in any way from the basics of the game they know, most casual players seem more than fine with the trade-off in return for the convenience of playing on the go. In WWF, premium squares have been placed elsewhere on the board; there are 104 tiles compared to Scrabble's 100 (including an extra E, T, S, and D, which makes play somewhat easier); and the value of about half the letters have been tweaked.

To many, the biggest difference (and bone of contention) between Words With Friends and Scrabble is not the point values or the rearranged board, but that Words With Friends adheres to an alternate dictionary. It follows the Enhanced North American Benchmark Lexicon (ENABLE), a list used by many other electronic board games. While most of the words in this book are also found in ENABLE, many (like **qi** and **za**) are not. However, Words With Friends is to be commended for openly offering users the chance to offer suggestions for edits to ENABLE (**qi** and **za**, which were originally excluded, are now both playable in WWF).

With the Lexulous lawsuit, Hasbro realized the value of a web-based version of Scrabble, and redoubled its efforts to create a viable, official digital version. It contracted with GameHouse, which created an aesthetically pleasing electronic version that faithfully replicated the actual game of Scrabble. Unfortunately, it didn't allow for online play and came with a $19.95 price tag, as opposed to the ad-based but essentially free versions of Scrabulous/Lexulous and Words With Friends. Though it was ideal for at-home play against a computer opponent, the GameHouse version never caught on. Hasbro turned to Electronic Arts (EA) for a mobile app game, which it released in 2008. Where the GameHouse version limited its lexicon to words appearing in the *OSPD*, EA's game offers the choice of either playing by words listed in the *OSPD* or the *Official Tournament and Club Word List* (OWL), the complete and official word list used in competitive Scrabble, as well as Lexulous. (OWL contains all the words in the *OSPD*, plus a list of longer and expunged words left out of the dictionary. For more on the difference between the OWL and the *OSPD*, see History of the Scrabble Lexicon on page 38.)

The EA version allows for play against multiple opponents as well as a computer opponent, and creates player skill ratings. Using Facebook, one can restrict the pool of random opponents by rating. And the mobile app allows one to play Scrabble Duplicate (see Scrabble in France, page 38)—a surprising if widely ignored option. While Hasbro got off to a late start in offering a viable mobile Scrabble app, the advantage of presenting the actual game has won it a rapidly expanding following. But with its competitions' loyal fan bases, the future of online and mobile play is anybody's game.

LOST A LETTER? PICKING UP SCRABBLE, PIECEMEAL

Hasbro won't sell you a single letter—no matter how badly you may want an extra K to form **tokamak** (a donut-shaped nuclear reactor, also **tokomak**) without a blank—but it does currently offer all 100 tiles, four racks, and a tile pouch for $6.50. And they'll sell you a new game board (strangely, called a "gameboard" on the order form on the Hasbro website, though gameboard is not playable) for $5. A scorepad (which—you guessed it!—is written *score pad* on the order form although **scorepad** is playable) is $2.50, and instructions are free. So the whole contents of a Scrabble box can be yours for $14. As Scrabble often sells for $20 to $25, that cardboard box may be the most valuable part!

Scrabble in France

Competitive Scrabble is played the world over, generally in tournaments that pair competitors in one-on-one play. However, in France, Quebec, and other *frenchified* places, tournament Scrabble takes the form of *le Scrabble Duplicate*, a form of the game created to eliminate chance. Players sit alone, each at his own board, facing the front of the room where oversize letters are drawn and announced. Each player attempts to make the highest-scoring play with those letters, and is awarded the number of points that their play would earn. The highest-scoring play is then selected and applied to the oversize board in the front of the room, and each player, regardless of what he played on his last turn, applies that same highest-scoring play to his own board. Then new tiles are chosen in the front corresponding to however many tiles were used on the last move, and each player endeavors to find the best play with those new letters on that same board.

On one hand, there can be no more whining about luck: everyone has the same board and letters to work with. On the other hand, aspects of the game such as defense or saving some letters to use on the next turn (so-called rack management) are meaningless here. In his book, *How to Play Scrabble Like a Pro*, world champion Joel Wapnick opines, "Le Scrabble Duplicate is to North American Scrabble what a foul-shooting contest is to basketball." Swish!

History of the Scrabble Lexicon

From the time Alfred Mosher Butts created Lexiko in the 1930s through its transformation in the 1950s into the modern, standardized form of

Scrabble as we now know it, Scrabble was primarily a friendly game, a "parlor" game.

But in the 1960s, gamers in the chess clubs in Manhattan—where chess, checkers, backgammon, and Go players would meet for serious competition—started taking the game to a competitive level. In smoky rooms, regulars challenged each other to timed, penny-a-point matches that increasingly played out at unprecedented levels of calculation, skill, and tenacity, involving ever-rarer words and higher scores. (Think of this as the age when Scrabble players went from playing **cat** to **kat**.) These highly skilled "sharks" used handicaps (maybe spotting opponents 50 points, or handicapping their own allotted time) to lure in "fish," casual players off the street who often didn't quite know what they were in for.

Remember, this was a time when Scrabble's popularity was soaring, and new, niche versions of the game were popping up in social circles around the country. Once money became involved, some rules of play needed to be sorted out. Scrabble sets came—as they still do—with box-top rules, but aspects of the game like players' ability to challenge questionable words, timed play, and a standardized list of acceptable words were missing.

The standard lexicon became *Funk & Wagnalls College Dictionary*, the principal dictionary of the day. (The book was also the source of much mirth on the television show *Rowan and Martin's Laugh-In*, where the line "Go look it up in your *Funk and Wagnalls*" became an oft-repeated joke, playing on the sound of "funk.") But *Funk & Wagnalls* had some serious organizational shortcomings when used for Scrabble play. In 1973, work began on an official dictionary for Scrabble. Words were culled from five dictionaries: *Random House College Dictionary* (1968), *American Heritage Dictionary of the English Language* (1969), *Webster's New World Dictionary* (2nd edition, 1970), *Webster's Collegiate* (1973), and *Funk & Wagnalls Standard College Dictionary* (1973). In 1978 the *Official Scrabble Players Dictionary* (OSPD) was officially adopted. The compilers, though paid, received no credit in the dictionary. Occasionally one finds definitions in the OSPD that seem inexplicable. In *Letterati*, Paul McCarthy reports that one of the two compilers of the original OSPD recalls including "some definitions that were inside jokes that only they understood."

As the dictionary's purpose was to list playable words in a condensed format, definitions were necessarily brief and vague. Of course, there were also a lot of unusual entries. One of which, **rei**, is defined as "an erroneous English form for a former Portuguese coin." Isn't privelege an erroneous form of **privilege**? Why include an incorrectly **spelt** word?

The first *OSPD* was a giant leap forward, but it was still found to lack many words. An improved second edition came out in 1991. It was very much the result of work by a dedicated man named Joe Leonard, who reportedly submitted more than 5,500 omissions and errors. He never asked for pay, and never received any. Nor did he receive any credit in the 1991 or subsequent editions, though he is currently recognized on the North American Scrabble Players Association site (Scrabbleplayers.org).

YOU CAN'T PLAY THAT ON TELEVISION: EXPUNGING THE *OSPD*

The cover of the second *OSPD* boasted that the new edition contained "over 3,000 new entries." While its predecessor included the likes of **shit** and *fuck* (it even included that unholy of unholies, **cunt**), the second edition added entries like **shithead** and *fuckup* and words like the rather humorous **bazooms**. This isn't to imply that it added 3,000 "dirty" words, but rather that the publisher, Merriam-Webster, and the producers of Scrabble, at that point Milton Bradley, weren't shy or deeply censorious of the game's official word list. And like the first edition, the second included a host of often abhorrent racial slurs; a surprisingly extensive list of insults that, if one were pressed to commend it for some reason, could only be praised for being so wide-ranging in its scope: Black or white or brown or yellow, male or female, gentile or Jew, just about everyone was represented and abused. It was all in there, so much of the English language, from its prettiest, most poetic, and uplifting to the foulest, most disgraceful, and contemptible. To signify the vulgar and/or odious natures of some of the words included in the first two *OSPD*s, the three-word disclaimer "an offensive term" was pinned to the end of their definitions.

THE J-ISH QUESTION

Growing up playing Scrabble in a Jewish family in the 1980s, I remember being aware of some of these offensive words. Of course, a child's eyes are invariably drawn to four-letter words—even as an adult I sometimes thrill at seeing a dirty word in a respectable place like a dictionary. But I also remember seeing words that were so obviously offensive and taboo that I felt no thrill, only somehow a sense of shame at even spotting them, knowing very well I'd never dare try to play them.

As a Jew, I knew **hebe** and **yid** were offensive in a theoretical sense, but having never been called either of those words, let alone in a hateful way, and having a general feeling of ownership of those words, I felt **okeh** (okay) playing them. My parents may have encountered the words in an offensive way when they were younger, but if they did, a certain feeling of ownership allowed for their use on the board—at least in comparison to a pragmatism associated with wanting to win. But then there was the "k" word—**kike**—which cannot but ring in the ear in a positively hateful, loathsome way. (Well, to my family's ears anyway.) Luckily, playing that word would require having the K and the blank at the same time, and if by some chance you had that, odds were good you could do something a far sight better with that rack.

So that leaves the great ponderable of my Scrabble playing as a youth: **jew**. It would've been one thing if *jew* had been defined as a noun, as in a Jew, but as a proper noun that could not be the case. Instead, it was "*Jew*: to bargain with—an offensive term." Offensive all right, I could see that. The idea of using it in speech like that seemed in some ways even worse than *kike*. At least with *kike*, the message seemed to be fairly matter of fact: "You are a Jew. (And I don't like you because of that fact so I call you this name.)" But with *jew* it was "I think so lowly of Jews I'll use their name to insult someone who isn't even Jewish. And that person will be degraded by my comparing his behavior to a Jew's." So terrible! And yet . . . and yet . . . look at those points! How often would one get stuck with the J and see that W out there on the board, flapping in the breeze. Or vice versa: there'd be that J, and here I was with an E and a W, and maybe there was a Double Word Score involved, and if I didn't use it someone else was surely ready to make

Eating Your Words: Playable Candy Names

Bonbon: a type of chocolate-coated sweet

Butterfingers: a clumsy person (also **butterfingered**, but not butterfinger)

Candyfloss: cotton candy

Fireball: a ball of fire, a meteor

Jawbreaker: a type of hard candy

Jujube: a type of edible berry (*not to be confused with* **juju**: *an object believed to have mystical powers*)

Nestle: to lie close to something or someone

Skittle: a form of bowling, or a pin used in that game

Starburst: an image resembling a diffusion of light

Tootsie: a foot (also **tootsy**)

Whatchamacallit: something whose name one cannot remember or does not know

jo or **jet** or **jot** or **jut** and pick up those points just *sitting* there!

And so it was that depending on one's letters and the board and the score sheet, *jew*, despite the intended and understood offense, was turned into offence. You'd play it, you'd lay those letters down, but you wouldn't say it. You'd just click those tiles into place and look up and say your score, generally "26," and you'd be met with everyone else's eyes, eyes saying "really?" And you'd look back at them knowing that they'd probably do the same, in which case you'd give them the "really?" look, too. And then *jew* would sit there on the board. And it wasn't all that rare that someone would then go on to play *jew* off another side of the same J later in the game if he or she could. (A play I like to think of as a "**jujube**.")

Scrabble's relationship with offensive words has been complicated as well. Take for example an event from 1990. Bob Felt had just won the National Scrabble Championship, and was a guest on *Good Morning America* to show off his winning board and define some of the words he played. Unbeknownst to the audience, Felt fiddled with the board, changing *darkies* to **darkens**. "I didn't think that defining that word on national television was in anybody's interest," he said later.

And yet there were these words, prescribed and described for all to see in the *OSPD*. That is, until 1993, when Virginia art gallery owner Judith Grad discovered just a few of the multitude of shockingly offensive terms in the *OSPD*. She was incensed. She dispatched letters to Merriam-Webster, that published the dictionary, and Milton Bradley, that headed Hasbro's games division.

"It is certainly not the intent of the dictionary to perpetuate racial or ethnic slurs or to make such usages respectable," read the response from Merriam-Webster's editor in chief. "However, such slurs are part of the language and reputable dictionaries record them as such."

"As a dictionary, it is a reflection of words currently used in our language," replied Milton Bradley's President. He added, "It is important to note that Milton Bradley Co. does not condone the use of these words, nor do we advocate the use of offensive terms. If it were up to us, none of these words—nor the sentiments behind them—would exist at all."

Unsatisfied, Grad reached out to groups including the Anti-Defamation League and the National Association for the Advancement of Colored People, still with no result. The National Council of Jewish Women, however, launched a letter-writing campaign, and then the Anti-Defamation League (ADL) amped up its efforts. An ADL chairman insisted on the removal of the offending words. "The use of ethnic slurs in Scrabble," he wrote Hasbro, "is literally playing games with hate." Not only were many players suddenly declaring their discomfort with playing some words in the OSPD, but there was also the immediate chance of a major black eye for the Scrabble brand—not to mention the consideration for the Scrabble in Schools initiative that had begun.

Meanwhile, though some competitive players were pleased by the prospect of ridding the game of some of its nastier bits, many argued that the words in the OSPD were like chess pieces: meaningless objects used to play a game. They'd studied and mastered these pieces, and it was ridiculous for Hasbro to strip them of these tools because some parlor players were, to their minds, overly sensitive. Besides, once one started to purge the lexicon, where would it end?

A PAX SCRABBALLA: THE *OSPD*, *OWL*, THE LL, AND SOWPODS

In an unusual compromise between many competitive players' wishes to keep the *OSPD* free of censorship and Hasbro's corporate concerns to escape bad press and remain family and school friendly, it was announced at the 1994 National Scrabble Championship that there would be two lists. The third *OSPD* would be expurgated for home and school use. A separate list for competitive use, the *Official Tournament and Club Word List* (alternately abbreviated as *OWL*, *TWL*, and *OCTWL*—leave it to Scrabble players to come up with three terms for the same thing!) would remain uncensored. The *OWL* was to be available only to members of the National Scrabble Association (NSA), but this has proven impossible to enforce, and it can be readily purchased online.

When the third *OSPD* came out in 1996, players sleuthing through the book found that a total of 167 words had been expunged, including not just the obviously offensive slurs and sex acts, but more questionable choices, too. Both **papist** (a Roman Catholic—an offensive term) and **nonpapist** (apparently similarly—though oppositely—offensive) were cut, as were **jesuit** (a scheming person—an offensive term) (*who knew?*), **fatso**, **libber** (one who supports a liberation movement), **comsymp** (one who sympathizes with the communist movement), **spaz**, **poo**, and **fart**. Also struck from the book were a myriad of trademarked words, such as **biro**, **jacuzzi**, **lycra**, **pyrex**, and **tofutti**. The list has come to be known by competitive players as "The *Poo* List." For a complete list (not recommended for sensitive eyes), visit this book's companion website at Isthatascrabbleword.com.

Meanwhile, the *OWL* is a book-length list of all the words of up to nine letters long that are permitted in sanctioned play. It contains everything: the lewd and the crude; the racist, xenophobic, and homophobic; and the potentially trademarked. Devoid of definitions, it keeps Scrabble delightfully disconnected from whatever those nasty words might mean, while offering a coolly calculated embrace of the idea that, for competitive Scrabble players, the words are detached from any denotation or connotation.

For international competition, players use a lexicon known as SOWPODS, which is an acronym composed of *OSPD* and the *OWL* from the name of the British lexicon, the British Official Word List. SOWPODS is therefore considerably larger than the *OSPD* and contains all of the words in the Long List (LL).

Downloadable as a .txt file at www.scrabbleplayers.org, the NSA website, the LL provides the full list of inflected words of ten to fifteen letters (the longest length word a standard Scrabble board can accommodate), beyond what even the *OWL* provides. For instance, while *OWL* lists **abiogenic**, the LL includes **abiogenically**. Where else would one come across such a lovely word as **kittenishnesses**, explain

"Dirty" Words That Remain in the *OSPD* under Alternative Definitions

Poop is in the *OSPD*, defined not as excrement but as "to make exhausted"; **pee** refers to the letter; **dick** in the sense of a detective; **dicker** is to haggle. **Pussy** is a cat, or as a less attractive word: the adjective meaning "full of puss." **Cock** is to tilt to the side and **cum** is the preposition meaning "along with." **Tit** squeaked into the *OSPD* as a little bird; **titty**'s there in a more mammary or agrarian sense, a sophomoric one as "a teat"; **tittie** is defined as "a sister." Personally, I don't think it's **crappy**—that is to say, decidedly bad—that **crapola**, meaning utter nonsense, remains a legit bingo possibility.

The **tit**'s **tittie**, a **tomtit** in a **titfer**, watches the **titman tittup** to the **titty**, **whilst** the **ouistiti** with **otitis** and the **bushtit titter** over the **titbit** of **titian tittle**, because they were **boobies**.

Tit: a type of little bird

Tittie: a sister

Tomtit: any of various types of little birds

Titfer: a hat (*British slang*)

Titman: the smallest piglet in a litter (pl. -men)

Tittup: to move in an exaggerated or jerky way

Titty: a teat

Whilst: while

Ouistiti: a marmoset (*sometimes also called* <u>wistit</u>, *but sadly that variation is not playable*)

Otitis: inflammation of the ear

Bushtit: a titmouse

Titter: to laugh in a partially suppressed way, to giggle

Titbit: a tidbit

Titian: a bright auburn color (*derived from Titian, who was fond of painting in this color, particularly women with red hair*)

Tittle: a small diacritical mark in writing or typography, as in the dot above a lowercase *i*

Booby: a fool (pl. **boobies**)

to an inquiring opponent that *tsutsugamushis* are bacteria that form a type of typhus (and are found primarily in an area—located between northern Japan, northern Australia, and Pakistan—known as the "*tsutsugamushi* triangle"), or ponder the irony of playing **nonachievements** across the board, perhaps even across three Triple Word Scores.

Two fifteen-letter (quidralettral?) words have been played in tournament play: Ken Clark put the *re* in **reconsideration** in 1990, and Ed Liebfried put the *dis* in **discontentments** in 2005.

OFFENSIVE WORDS THAT HAVE NOT BEEN EXPUNGED

Despite Hasbro's august efforts to expunge offensive words from the *OSPD*, somehow several escaped the scythe. A black urban professional can refer to himself as a **buppy** (or **buppie**), and **ponce** ("to pimp"), **fem** ("a passive homosexual"), **nelly/nellie** ("an effeminate male"), and **butch** ("a lesbian with mannish traits") can still be played in living rooms across America. So can **bumpkin** ("an unsophisticated rustic"), **hayseed** ("a bumpkin"), and **hick** ("a rural person"). The definition of **sambo** ("a Latin American of mixed black and Indian ancestry") disregards its most common usage as a slur.

Perhaps even more troubling, despite complaints from Romanies, **gyp** ("to swindle") and **gypper** ("one that gyps") are legal. How this differs from using *jew* in the same way is hard to imagine. Then again, **rom** ("a Gypsy man or boy") is also allowed, despite its near-universal capitalization in English. Again, why this cultural group earns the distinction of being declassified from proper-noun status is bewildering.

Other words derived from places or ethnicities that one might point to as offensive are also listed in the *OSPD*: **mongol** ("a person affected with a form of mental deficiency"—also **mongolian, mongoloid**, and **mongolism**), **oriental** ("an inhabitant of an eastern country"), and **shanghai** ("to kidnap for service aboard a ship") come to mind. **Cyprian** ("a prostitute"—derived from the ancient orgiastic worship of Aphrodite on Cyprus) and **paphian** ("a prostitute"— derived from Paphos, an ancient Cypriot city) seem odd choices not to strike.

Truly, the path of expurgation is a difficult one to navigate, and quickly becomes a slippery slope. The trailblazer's task of determining what trees to fell, what rocks and roots to uproot, and what bumps in the road to leave be is not to be envied, and perhaps it is too easy at times to criticize. But when that path becomes a highway, or else major obstacles to its destination (some happy place where people are not made to feel excluded or insulted) are left intact, it seems right to call attention to it.

Personally, I'm all for playing with every dirty word one can think of. And I'm also all for playing without them. Competitive Scrabble players, for their part, like to say that the tiles are not the pieces in Scrabble; it's the words that are the pieces. To my mind, as long as my opponent and I decide on which set of words/pieces to use (be it the *OSPD* or the *OWL*), it's fine with me. But I also understand that each Scrabble player should have the right to make that decision. So I would urge Hasbro to make a version of the *OWL*, with definitions included, easily available to the public. And it's to be hoped that each future edition of the *OSPD* will strive to correct the oversights as well as overzealousnesses of its predecessors, just as it's up to all speakers of any language to do the same in their usage.

The Sound of Muzjik
Scrabble Records

It's said that records are meant to be broken, but some records are meant to be played. In Scrabble, records for the highest-scoring plays and games are kept only for matches officially sanctioned by the National Scrabble Association—typically in Scrabble clubs or tournaments.

The highest-scoring-possible seven-letter opening play is a bingo that comes from the letters IJKMSUZ, which look unpromising unless you recognize **muzjiks**. Placing the Z on the Double Letter Score is an opening move that would bring in 128 points. The odds of drawing these tiles are about 1 in 55 million, and indeed the play has never been recorded in sanctioned play. However, Jesse Inman of South Carolina did open a game at the 2008 National Scrabble Championships with **muzjiks** using the blank for the U for a record-setting 126-point opening move.

Muzjiks is a pluralized, alternative spelling of the equally impressive though slightly lower-scoring **muzhik**, a Russian peasant, particularly a serf before the Russian Revolution of 1917. **Muzhik** came into

English thanks in large part to Tolstoy and Dostoyevsky; the latter even penned a seemingly autobiographical, <u>Slavophilic</u> short story about a kind muzhik he knew as a child, the title of which is translated alternatively as "The Peasant Marey" or "The Muzhik Marey." Today, *muzhik* is used in Russian as the equivalent of "guy" or "dude."

While the chance of ever playing **muzjiks** is unlikely, drawing IJKMSUV from the bag is as likely as getting wet when it's raining out in comparison to pulling **muumuu(s)** (with a blank for the s) on your first turn. It's the least-likely opening bingo out there, and at a staggering 8 billion to 1 shot, the 76 points seem like a paltry reward. Personally, I'm in favor of having a special "MUUMUU Move" muumuu made, to be awarded to anyone who has such amazing luck.

The second-highest opening move ever recorded in American tournament play is **bezique** (a card game similar to pinochle) for 124 points. **Cazique** (a tropical oriole) and **mezquit** (a shrub found throughout the American Southwest, also spelled **mesquit, mesquite**) would also bring in that much.

If you like to dream big, the next-highest valued monster openings would be:

122 POINTS

Kolhozy: a Russian collective farm
Sovkhoz: a state-owned farm found in the former Soviet Union

Zinkify: to cover with zinc (also **zincify**)
Zombify: to transform into a zombie

120 POINTS

Jazzily: in a jazz-like way
Jezebel: an evil woman
Jukebox: a machine that plays recorded music for money
Muzhiks: Russian peasants
Quetzal: a tropical bird
Quezals: quetzals

Quickly: in short time
Quizzed: tested for information
Squeeze: to hold tightly
Squiffy: inebriated
Zymurgy: the study of fermentation into alcohol

a Jukebox
b Quetzal
c Jezebel
d Muzhiks
e Squiffy

OTHER RECORDS

The most record-breaking game of sanctioned Scrabble in North America took place on October 12, 2006, in Lexington, Massachusetts. Michael Cresta of Massachusetts set two records, for a single turn with **quixotry** for 365 points and for total points with 830. His opponent, Wayne Yorra, put up 490 points himself, helping set the record for highest combined score with 1,320.

DOUBLE- AND TRIPLE-TRIPLES

Beziques, **caziques**, **mezquite**, **mezquits**, and **oxazepam** also tie for the highest possible eight-letter bingos. If placed across two Triple Word Scores—known as a double-triple—each can be played for 392 points.

The holy grail of Scrabble is the triple-triple (sometimes referred to as a triple-triple-triple), a play that spans three Triple Word Scores. There's no record of a triple-triple ever having been played.

Theoretically, the highest possible move in Scrabble has been determined to be **oxyphenbutazone** (an anti-inflammatory used to treat arthritis) played as a triple-triple. There's much debate about

You're Prequalified!

At first glance it seems ridiculous that *oxyphenbutazone* is permitted in Scrabble but prequalified isn't—after all, prequalified is a term one hears fairly often in talk of loans. But prequalification has generally been hyphenated, appearing as pre-qualified. Further, the mind reels a bit at the idea of prequalification as opposed to qualification. That *pre-* does seem, well, if not redundant, at least utterly useless. Although then again there is the case of Formula One racing, which for a time utilized a "pre-qualifying" round to determine who would get to compete in the "qualifying" round, which in turn decided who would be allowed to ultimately compete in a race. Better yet, one could argue that this sidebar prequalifies the reader to weigh in on the topic, even without the qualifications of being an expert on the subject.

how much this word can score, depending on whether one uses *OWL* or *SOWPODS* words to construct the ideal opening for the word on the board. (It boils down to the fact that *OWL* does not permit prequalified—a necessary play to create a slightly higher-scoring **oxyphenbutazone** than without it—though SOWPODS does.) It's a puzzle many folks are continuing to work on. Suffice it to say that either way, the nearly 1,800 points one could score would be one for the record books. The highest combined score for a theoretical game using only *OWL* words is approximately 4,000 points.

THE LONGEST GAME (WITH THE SHORTEST MOVES)

In a 1993 tournament in Tennessee, Jan Dixon and Paul Avrin played a game in which they each took twenty-five turns, which averages to exactly two tiles per play.

FIVE POINTS PER SECOND: THE SHORTEST GAME

In a 2003 tournament in New Jersey, Scrabble expert Matt Graham played a complete game in 96 seconds, scoring 471 points. So much for not wanting to play Scrabble "because it takes so long"; that's a whole game of turns taking about as long as it does to sneeze a few times.

"Achoo! Ahchoo!"

"Kerchoo!"

"Gesundheit!"

THE GREATEST MOVE . . . EVER?

The play that is often cited as the most impressive word ever played in Scrabble took place in 1995. Jim Geary, a former pro poker player, was down by 90 and holding BEEIORW with two letters left in the bag. He calculated that if he played off his B and an E, there was a $\frac{1}{68}$ chance he could pick up an A and a T, which were either in the bag or on his opponent's rack. The odds played out in Geary's favor: he pulled the A and T, and with a rack of AEIORTW he played through a Z and an O on the board to end the game with **waterzooi**, a classic Flemish stew with fish or chicken. It scored 92 points, plus the value of his opponent's rack.

LESS THAN ZERO: WINNING WITH NEGATIVE POINTS

The record for the lowest winning score ever is currently held by Helena Gauthier, who beat her opponent: –9 to –11. How does something like this happen? Let's take a look at a game that set the previous record of –8 points, set back in 1990.

At the start of a game at the Midwest Invitational Tournament in July, 1990, Rod Nivison's first rack was UNIDEAE. His opponent picked seven tiles, and as he did so accidentally exposed one tile to Nivison: the D. Rod saw the opportunity for **unidead** (ironically, it means "without ideas"), and so he passed, hoping his opponent would play that D. His opponent traded in a tile, so Rod passed again. His opponent traded in another tile, and Rod passed again. His opponent played the phony <u>dormine</u> (**minored** would have worked) and Rob challenged it off the table.

At the time, the rules clearly stated that game play ended if both players scored 0 points (through passing or trading in tiles) three times in a row. The rule made sense, because it was a clear way to stop play at the end of a game, when players might not be able—or want—to put down any tiles, and was fashioned—like several other Scrabble rules—after a rule in chess. It was simply unforeseen that it might be invoked so early in the game.

Each player then subtracted the value of his own tiles from his score (which was 0 to 0 at the time), and Nivison came out the winner, –8 to –10.

Sometimes in Scrabble, less is more.

PART 2

Unscrambling Scrabblish:
A Catalog of Useful, Curious, and Surprising Lists, Facts, and Marginalia

Since the earliest Scrabble players first started perusing the *Funk & Wagnalls* dictionary for words that could aid their game, generations of players have sought to systemize their efforts to improve their chances of winning by enlarging their vocabulary. While these efforts often include long lists of words organized alphabetically by their anagrams, some players prefer words grouped together thematically. Here's a look at some of the game's lexicon presented through a combination of connected words and peculiar trivia from playable band names to unusual terms for body parts.

"Biblically Speaking . . ."
Words from the Bible

The *OSPD* may be the Scrabble players' **bible**, but plenty of words found there have their roots in the original Good Book (if not always their definitions).

> In the **noel**, the light from the **lucifer** through the **judas** gives the **magdalen** in a **joseph** a **gloria**, as if illuminating the **ruth** of her **saul**.

Noel: a Christmas card
Lucifer: a friction match
Judas: a peephole
Magdalen: a former prostitute
Joseph: a woman's long cloak (*after Joseph's coat of many colors*)
Gloria: a halo
Ruth: compassion
Saul: a soul

OTHER PLAYABLE BIBLICAL WORDS INCLUDE:

Bible: a definitive text
Calvary: a representation of the crucifixion
Golgotha: a burial place
Jezebel: an evil woman
Lazar: a beggar afflicted with a terrible disease, particularly a leper
Maria: a large plain on the surface of the moon that appears dark

Sodom: a place infamous for vice
Torah: a law (pl. **torahs**, **toroth**, or **torot**)
Veronica: a handkerchief with a depiction of Christ's face (*after the Biblical woman who offered Jesus a handkerchief to wipe his face as he carried his cross*)

Toponyms
Finding the Right Place on the Board

The names of specific places, languages, or geographically grouped peoples (Russia, Hebrew, Parisians) are **verboten** (not permitted) in Scrabble, as they are proper nouns. However, *toponymic* words named after places are often legal. One can feel free to eat a **danish** off **china** plates while wearing a **kashmir** sweater, a **panama** hat, and a pair of **bermudas**, and it's okay by the *OSPD*. (Even though it's likely that the danish originated in Vienna and panama hats first came from Ecuador, but that's another story.) After you do the **german**, you can sit in your **berlin**, wrapped in **alaska**, smoke something **colorado**, and play **boston**.

Afghan: a wool blanket

Alamo: a cottonwood poplar tree

Alaska: "a heavy fabric," according to the *OSPD* (*presumably this refers to wool from Alaska, perhaps* **qiviut**, *wool from the Alaskan musk ox*)

Berlin: a type of fancy, fast, and light horse-drawn carriage (*later,* **berline** *came to be used for early limousines*)

Bermudas: a variety of knee-length, wide-legged shorts

Bohemia: a community of unconventional, usually artistic, people

Bolivia: "a soft fabric" according to the *OSPD* (*like* **alaska**, *another noun for a type of fabric that has disappeared from many dictionaries*)

Bordeaux: wine from the Bordeaux region

Boston: a card game similar to whist

Brazil: a type of tree found in Brazil used to make instrument bows (also **brasil**)

Brit: a non-adult herring

Cayman: a type of **croc** (a crocodile), also known as a spectacled crocodile (also **caiman**)

Celt: a type of ax used during the New Stone Age

Chile: a spicy pepper (also **chili**)

Colorado: used to describe cigars of medium strength and color

Congo: "an eellike amphibian" in the *OSDP* (*There are types of frogs and snakes called congo, and a common type of eel*

called the **conger**, *but traces of an* **eellike**—*good word!*—*amphibian by this name escape my investigations.*)

Cyprus: "a thin fabric," according to the *OSPD* (*Silk has long been an export of Cyprus, since the* **bombyx**—*a silkworm*—*was imported from China.*)

Dutch: referring to each person paying for himself

Egyptian: a sans serif typeface

English: to cause a ball to spin

French: to slice food thinly

Gambia: a flowering plant also known as uncaria or cat's claw (also **gambier**, *which happens to be a small town in Ohio*)

Geneva: gin, or a liquor like gin (*Gin is often cited as a shortened form of* **geneva**, *which is likely derived from* genièvre, *the French word for juniper.*)

Genoa: a type of **jib** (a triangular sail), also known as a **jenny**, first used by a Swedish sailor in Genoa

German: also known as the german **cotillon**, an elaborate nineteenth-century dance, which sometimes involved having to jump over a rope just to get onto the dance floor

Greek: something not understood

Guinea: a type of British coin minted from 1663 to 1813

Holland: a linen fabric

Japan: to gloss with black lacquer (*One can even* **japanize china.**)

Java: coffee

Jordan: a chamber pot (*see Shakespeare's* Henry IV: *"Why, they will allow us ne'er a jordan, and then we leak in your chimney."*)

Kashmir: cashmere

Mecca: a destination for many people

Oxford: a type of formal men's shoe, also known as a **bal** or **balmoral**

Panama: a type of wide-brimmed hat

Paris: a type of plant found in Europe and Asia that produces a lone, poisonous berry

Roman: a romance written in meter

Scot: an assessed tax (*Think of* "scot-free.")

Scotch: to put an end to; or to etch or scratch (as in **hopscotch**)

Sherpa: a soft fabric used for linings

Siamese: a water pipe providing a connection for two hoses

Swiss: a sheer, cotton fabric

Texas: a tall structure on a steamboat containing the pilothouse

Toledo: a type of sword famous for its fine craftsmanship, originally from Toledo

Wale: to injure, to create welts

on the skin

Warsaw: a type of grouper fish

Waterloo: a definitive defeat

Zaire: a currency of Zaire

Sing, O Muse, of Those Ingenious Words That Have Traveled Far and Wide from Ancient Greece to the Scrabble Board

Familiarity with the names and places associated with the **Iliad** and the **Odyssey** will serve one well in Scrabble. And although we can sit and wish that Aeaea (the mythical island said to be the home of the sorceress Circe) were playable, **Homer**'s two **epically** great poems certainly do offer Scrabble players some godlike powers.

Achillea: an herb, also known as **yarrow**

Acropolis: a citadel

Aeneus: greenish-gold in color (also **aeneous**)

Aphrodite: a type of orange-colored butterfly of North America; also a type of orchid

Apollo: a handsome man

Ares: plural of **are**: a unit of surface measure equal to 100 square meters

Arete: a sharp, narrow mountain ridge

Argosy: a large merchant ship or

a fleet of such ships

Artemisia: a plant belonging to the daisy family used in herbal medicine

Atheneum: a literary or scientific institution

Calypso: a style of music from the West Indies, usually with improvised lyrics

Cyclopes: a tiny (½- to 3-mm) crustacean with a single, central eye (also **cyclops**) (**Cyclopes** *was erroneously omitted from some editions of the* OSPD.)

Hector: to bully, usually verbally

Homer: to hit a homerun in baseball

Homeric: having an impressively large or grand quality

Iliad: a lengthy poem, often describing a series of misfortunes

Ilium: the upper part of either of the innominate bones of the pelvis

Muse: to think about

Nestor: a wise, elderly man

Odyssey: a long, adventure-filled journey

Phoenix: a mythical bird said to have lived in the Arabian desert for 500 years, cyclically burning itself to death and emerging anew from its own ashes

Stento: a person with a strong voice

Troy: a system of weights used primarily for gems and precious metals

Xenia: the effect of pollen on a plant (Xenia *is known to readers of Homer as the Greek term for hospitality. The botanic definition very likely derives from the Greek* **xenos**, *for "stranger."*)

It's Jabberwocky!

Jabberwocky, the title of Lewis Carroll's sensibly nonsensical poem included in *Through the Looking Glass, and What Alice Found There*, is a playable word defined in *Merriam-Webster*'s as "meaningless speech or writing." Although <u>brillig</u> cannot be played, many words from the poem do make the cut.

> 'Twas brillig, and the slithy toves
> Did **gyre** and gimble in the wabe;
> All mimsy were the borogoves,
> And the **mome raths** outgrabe.

> "Beware the Jabberwock, my son!
> The jaws that bite, the claws that catch!
> Beware the Jubjub bird, and shun
> The frumious Bandersnatch!"

He took his vorpal sword in hand:
Long time the manxome foe he sought—
So rested he by the Tumtum tree,
And stood awhile in thought.

And as in uffish thought he stood,
The Jabberwock, with eyes of flame,
Came **whiffling** through the tulgey wood,
And **burbled** as it came!

One, two! One, two! and through and through
The vorpal blade went snicker-snack!
He left it dead, and with its head
He went **galumphing** back.

"And hast thou slain the Jabberwock?
Come to my arms, my **beamish** boy!
O **frabjous** day! Callooh! Callay!"
He **chortled** in his joy.

'Twas brillig, and the slithy toves
Did gyre and gimble in the wabe;
All mimsy were the borogoves,
And the mome raths outgrabe.

While the first word of the poem, *'Twas*, is used as the contraction for "It was," **twas** is playable under another definition (it's the plural of **twa**, an alternative spelling of "two").

Gyre: to move in a circle or spiral
Mome: a fool
Rath: rathe, appearing or ripening early
Whiffle: "to move or think erratically," according to the *OSPD*

Burble: to speak quickly and excitedly
Galumph: to move clumsily
Beamish: cheerful
Frabjous: splendid
Chortle: to chuckle with glee

It seems likely that Carroll did not mean all of these words in the way they're defined by the *OSPD* (**mome** and **rath** in particular).

Just for fun, for those interested in something closer to Carroll's meaning (despite the fact that Carroll later offered contrary definitions), let's follow Alice's lead and consult Humpty Dumpty, who claimed he could "explain all the poems that ever were invented—and a good many that haven't been invented just yet."

"[T]here are plenty of hard words there. '*Brillig*' means four o'clock in the afternoon—the time when you begin *broiling* things for dinner."

"That'll do very well," said Alice: "and '*slithy*'?"

"Well, '*slithy*' means 'lithe and slimy.' 'Lithe' is the same as 'active.' You see it's like a portmanteau—there are two meanings packed up into one word."

"I see it now," Alice remarked thoughtfully: "and what are '*toves*'?"

"Well, '*toves*' are something like badgers—they're something like lizards—and they're something like corkscrews."

"They must be very curious-looking creatures."

"They are that," said Humpty Dumpty; "also they make their nests under sun-dials—also they live on cheese."

"And what's to '*gyre*' and to '*gimble*'?"

"To '*gyre*' is to go round and round like a gyroscope. To '*gimble*' is to make holes like a gimlet."

"And '*the wabe*' is the grass-plot round a sun-dial, I suppose?" said Alice, surprised at her own ingenuity.

"Of course it is. It's called '*wabe*' you know, because it goes a long way before it, and a long way behind it—"

"And a long way beyond it on each side," Alice added.

"Exactly so. Well, the '*mimsy*' is 'flimsy and miserable' (there's another portmanteau for you). And a '*borogove*' is a thin shabby-looking bird with its feathers sticking out all round—something like a live mop."

"And then '*mome raths*'?" said Alice. "I'm afraid I'm giving you a great deal of trouble."

"Well, a '*rath*' is a sort of green pig: but '*mome*' I'm not certain about. I think it's short for 'from home'—meaning that they'd lost their way, you know."

"And what does '*outgrabe*' mean?"

"Well, '*outgribing*' is something between bellowing and whistling, with a kind of sneeze in the middle: however, you'll hear it done, maybe—down in the wood yonder—and, when you've once heard it, you'll be *quite* content."

To Bingo, or Not to Bingo
Playable Shakespearean Characters

Some words with **bardic** (poetic) connections have roles to play on the board as well as on the stage:

Ariel: a gazelle found in Africa
Dogberry: the fruit of a dogwood tree
Hamlet: a village
Lear: learning
Puck: a disk used in ice hockey and other games
Romeo: a seductive male, a male lover
Shylock: to lend money with a high interest rate (considered offensive)

Other Standout Literary or Historical Eponyms

Bluebeard: a man who repeatedly marries and kills his wives

Caesar: an absolute leader
Einstein: an exceptionally intelligent person

Eyre: a long journey
Dickens: a devil (pl. -es)
Fagin: a person (usually an adult) who instructs others (often children) in crime
Holden: the past participle of **hold**
Huckleberry: a berry like a blueberry
Napoleon: a type of layered pastry
Oedipal: describing libidinal feelings of a child toward the parent of the opposite sex
Quixote: according to the *OSPD,* "a quixotic person" (*An interesting example of a noun being defined by an adjective derived from a proper noun.* **Quixotic** *is "extremely idealistic,"* **quixotry** *is "a quixotic action or thought."*)
Rousseau: fried pemmican (*Pemmican is a Native American high-protein, high-fat food composed of dried meat, occasionally mixed with fruit.*)
Zooey: like a zoo

Are You a Word?
Playable First Names

Al: a type of East Indian tree
Alan: a breed of hunting dog, named after the Alan people (also **aland**, **alant**)
Alec: a herring
Ana: a collection of miscellany about a specific topic
Anna: a former Indian coin
Barbie: a barbecue
Belle: a pretty woman
Ben: an inner room
Benny: an amphetamine pill
Bertha: a style of wide collar
Beth: a Hebrew letter
Biff: to hit
Bill: to charge for goods or services
Billy: a short club
Bo: a friend
Bobby: a policeman
Bonnie: pretty (also **bonny**)
Brad: a small nail or tack
Carl: a peasant or manual laborer (also **carle**)
Carol: to sing merrily
Celeste: a percussive keyboard instrument (also **celesta**)
Chad: a scrap of paper
Chevy: to chase (also **chivy**)
Christie: a type of turn in skiing (also **christy**)
Clarence: an enclosed carriage

Dagwood: a large, stuffed sandwich (*named after the comic strip character who was fond of them*)

Daphne: a flowering shrub with poisonous berries

Davy: a safety lamp

Deb: a debutante

Devon: a breed of cattle

Dexter: located to the right

Dom: a title given to some monks

Don: to put on a piece of clothing

Donna: an Italian woman of repute

Erica: a shrub of the heath family

Fay: to join together closely

Florence: a former European gold coin

Franklin: a nonnoble medieval English landowner

Fritz: a nonworking or semi-functioning state

Gilbert: a unit of magneto-motive force (*equal to $^{10}/_4\pi$ ampere-turn, in case you were wondering*)

Gilly: to transport on a type of train car

Graham: whole-wheat flour

Hank: to secure a sail

Hansel: to give a gift to, usually to commence a new year (also **handsel**)

Harry: to harass

Henry: a unit of electric inductance

Herby: full of herbs

Jack: to hoist with a type of lever

Jacky: a sailor

Jake: okay, satisfactory

Jane: a girl or woman

Jay: any of various birds, known for their crests and shrill calls

Jean: denim

Jenny: a female donkey

Jerry: a German soldier

Jess: to fasten a strap around the leg of a bird in falconry (also **jesse**)

Jill: a unit of liquid measure equal to ¼ of a pint

Jimmy: to pry open

Joannes: a Portuguese coin (also **johannes**)

Joe: a fellow

Joey: a young kangaroo

John: a toilet

Johnny: a hospital gown

Jones: a strong desire

Josh: to tease

Kelly: a bright shade of green

Kelvin: a unit of absolute temperature

Ken: to know

Kent: past tense of **ken**

Kerry: a breed of cattle

Kris: a curved dagger

Lars: plural of **lar**: a type of ancient Roman guardian

deity (also **lares**)
Lassie: a lass
Laura: an aggregation of her-
mitages used by monks
Laurel: to crown one's head
with a wreath
Lee: to shelter from wind
Louie: a lieutenant
Louis: a former gold coin of
France worth 20 francs
Mac: a raincoat
Mae: more
Mamie: a tropical, fruit-
bearing tree (also **mamey** and
mammee)
Marc: the pulpy residue of fruit
after it is pressed for wine
Marcel: to make waves in the
hair using a special iron
Marge: a margin
Martin: any of the type of bird
also known as a swallow
Marvy: marvelous
Matilda: a hobo's bundle
(*chiefly Australian, where the
hobo would likely be called a
swagman*)
Matt: to put a dull finish on
(also **matte**)
Maxwell: a unit of magnetic
flux
Mel: honey
Merle: a blackbird
Mickey: a drugged drink (*Also
known as a Mickey Finn, after a
Chicago bartender of that name
who, around the turn of the 20th*

*century, would slip some chloral
hydrate into unsuspecting
patrons' drinks, then bring the
incapacitated victims to a back
room where he would rob them.*)
Mike: a microphone
Milt: to fertilize with fish sperm
Minny: a minnow
Mo: a moment
Molly: a type of tropical fish
Morgan: a unit of frequency
in genetics
Morris: a type of folk dance
from England
Morse: describing a type of
code made of long and short
signals
Mort: a note sounded in hunt-
ing to announce the death
of prey
Nelson: a type of wrestling hold
Newton: the unit of force
required to accelerate one
kilogram of mass one meter
per second
Nick: to make a shallow cut
Norm: a standard
Pam: the name for the jack of
clubs in some card games
Peter: to lessen gradually
Pia: a fine membrane of the
brain and spinal chord
Randy: sexually excited
Regina: a queen
Rex: a king
Rick: to stack hay, corn, or straw
Rob: to steal

Robin: a type of thrush with a reddish breast

Rod: to provide with or use a rod

Roger: the pirate flag

Sal: salt

Sally: to make a brief trip or sudden start

Sawyer: one who saws wood

Shawn: past tense of *show*

Sheila: a girl or young woman

Sol: the fifth note of diatonic scale (also **so**)

Sonny: a boy or young man

Sophy: a former Persian ruler

Spencer: a type of sail

Tad: a young boy

Tammie: a fabric used in linings and curtains (also **tammy**)

Ted: to spread for drying

Teddy: a woman's one-piece undergarment

I Haint Afraid of No . . .

Banshee: a female spirit in Gaelic folklore that wails to warn of a family member's imminent death

Barguest: a goblin (also **barghest**)

Bogy: a goblin

Daimon: a spirit (also **daemon**)

Eidolon: a phantom or specter

Fairyism: the quality of being like a fairy (*not really a ghost, but a great word*)

Haint: a ghost

Kelpie: a water sprite in Scottish folklore known for drowning sailors

Wraith: a ghost of a person, often appearing just before that person's death

Zombi: a zombie (**Zombify** and **zombification** are both playable, *but are not to be confused with* **zombiism**, *a West African and Haitian belief system involving a rainbow serpent. See Wade Davis's* The Serpent and the Rainbow.)

Terry: a soft, absorbent type of cloth
Tiffany: a thin, mesh fabric
Timothy: a Eurasian grass used for grazing
Toby: a drinking mug in the shape of a man or a man's face
Tod: a British unit of weight for wool equal to 28 pounds
Tom: the male of various animals
Tommy: a loaf or chunk of bread
Tony: stylish
Vera: very
Victoria: a light, four-wheeled carriage
Warren: an area where rabbits live, or a crowded, mazelike place
Webster: one who weaves
Will: to choose, decree, or induce to happen
Willy: to clean fibers with a certain machine (also **willow**)

Trumping with Tramps

The world's oldest profession is also one of the best represented in the *OSPD*. Synonyms for **prostitute** abound in the dictionary. While the old classics like **hooker** and **whore** are included, here are ten less-familiar synonyms alongside some of their best usages:

Callet, as used in Shakespeare's *Othello*
> DESDEMONA: Am I that name, Iago?
> IAGO: What name, fair lady?
> DESDEMONA: Such as she says my lord did say I was.
> EMILIA: He call'd her whore; a beggar in his drink
> Could not have laid such terms upon his **callet**.
> IAGO: Why did he so?
> DESDEMONA: I do not know; I am sure I am none such.

Demirep, from *Tom Jones* by Henry Fielding
> "He had no knowledge of that character which is vulgarly called a **demirep**; that is to say, a woman who intrigues with every man she likes, under the name and appearance of virtue; and who, though some over-nice ladies will not be seen with her, is visited

(as they term it) by the whole town, in short, whom everybody knows to be what nobody calls her."

Quean: (pronounced "kwayne") from Lord Byron's *Don Juan*
"She was to dismiss her guards and he his Harem,
And for their other matters, meet and share 'em.

But as it was, his Highness had to hold
His daily council upon ways and means
How to encounter with this martial scold,
This modern Amazon, and queen of **queans**."

Trull: from Jonathan Swift's "A Proposal for Giving Badges to the Beggars of Dublin"
"If he be not quite maimed, he and his **trull**, and litter of brats (if he hath any) may get half their support by doing some kind of work in their power, and thereby be less burthensome to the people."

Other good ones include **chippy** (also **chippie**), **cocotte**, **cyprian**, **floozy** (also **floosy**, **floozie**, and **flossie**), and **pross** (also **prossie** and **prostie**).

Of course, there are plenty of other colorful words in the lexicon that deal with, **ahem**, the ins and outs of sex, or even interesting gender roles. Here are twenty-nine of them, including one of my favorite acceptable words, *pimpmobile*. (If you don't appreciate that such words are in the Scrabble lexicon, just remember: don't hate the **playa**, hate the game.)

Bawd: a female proprietress of a brothel

Bemadam: to refer to by the title of madam

Bimbette: an attractive but dumb young woman

Bimbo: a promiscuous woman, an unintelligent man

Catamite: a boy who is sodomized

Cathouse: a brothel

Cicisbeo: a lover of a married woman (pl. -beos, -beis) (*likely an inversion of the Italian* bel cece, *which translates literally to "beautiful chickpea," and*

*is used in the Italian in the
same way)*
Cornuto: a cuckold
Cotquean: a hussy, or a man
who busies himself in a house-
wife's affairs
Curiosa: pornographic
literature
Drab: to consort with
prostitutes
Frottage: the act of mastur-
bation by rubbing against
another person
Frotteur: one who engages
in frottage
Hoochie: a sexually promiscuous young woman
Lupanar: a brothel
Nudie: a film featuring
naked actors
Nympho: a woman with
extreme sexual desire
Peepshow: a performance,

generally sexual in nature,
watched through a small
hole
Pimp: to solicit clients for a
prostitute
Pimpmobile: an ostentatious
car characteristically owned
by a pimp
Playa: a basin in a desert valley
that may occasionally fill
with water
Porno: pornography
Porny: pornographic in nature
Rakehell: a man with little
moral restraint, a libertine
Sexpot: an extremely sexually
attractive woman
Sleazo: sleazy
Sleazoid: a sleazy person
Swive: to have sexual intercourse with
Tomcat: to be sexually promis-
cuous—used of men

It's Kosher for Scrabble
Yiddish Words My Grandmother Knew

The imminent death of <u>Yiddish</u>, a language that rivals <u>Scrabblish</u> for its lexicon of fantastic, unusual words, is a matter of much hand-wringing.

Players can **futz** with their letters while some little **pisher**, some **nudnik** across the table, **putzes** around with a blank. At the next table is some **schlemiel** who's **schlepped** his **schlock** in with him to bring him good luck. The **schlub** he's about to play **schlumps** in his chair, wiping his **schnoz** with a **schmatte**, and the two **schmos** sit and **schmooze** like a couple of **schmucks**. It's the same **shtick** every time, but at heart they're a couple of **nebbishy menschen**. When one makes a bingo, the other never says, "**oy**"—it's always "**mazeltov!**" without any **shmalz**.

Futz: to act ineffectually, either deliberately or inadvertently
Pisher: someone young and/or inexperienced

Nudnik: an obnoxious, annoying person (also **nudnick**) (*also the name by which each and every one of*

The Whole Schmeer

"Auto-antonyms" (or contronyms or antagonyms) are **homo-graphs** that have opposite meanings. Oft-cited examples include *left* (it can mean both "gone" or "still here"), *clip* ("to cut off" or "to attach together"), and *fast* ("to move quickly" and "to stay in one position"). **Schmeer**, which refers to a spread of butter or cream cheese on bread ("a bagel with a schmeer" is not uncommon parlance in New York City, to this day), can also be used as the verb "smear," as in, to apply a schmeer to a bagel (*schmeer* and *smear* share the same old German roots). It also means to "bribe," in the same sense as the English idiom "to butter up." Of course in English, *smear* is also to dishonor one's reputation, the opposite of buttering anyone up. So in a sense, in translation *schmeer*'s definitions are—if not opposites—at least oddly antithetical.

Schmeer can also be used in the sense of "everything together, or a little of everything together" as in, "What's he on trial for?— Oh, let's see: money laundering, racketeering, embezzlement, tax evasion . . . the whole schmeer." So while one can't schmeer someone in the sense of "to defame," one can schmeer (bribe) a politician with a schmeer (a large spread of cream cheese), or smear (defame) a politician for a schmeer of indecencies, including being a **ganef** (thief).

my Hebrew school teachers called me)

Putz: to deliberately act ineffectually (also slang for *penis*)

Schlemiel: a dope (also **schlemihl**)

Schlep: to carry laboriously or pitifully (also **schlepp**)

Schlock: worthless items (also **shlock**)

Schlub: a dumb or unfit person

Schlump: to move about lazily

Schnoz: the nose

Schmatte: a rag or garment of low quality

Schmo: a dolt (also **schmoe**) (from **schmuck**)

Schmooze: to speak idly or smoothly (also **schmoose**)

Schmuck: an obnoxious or stupid person (*literally* penis, from the Polish smok, *meaning "dragon"*)

Shtick: a routine (also **schtick**, **schtik**)

Nebbishy: meek (*describes a person who's a* **nebbish**)

Mensch: a good person (pl. -es, -en) (*The opposite of a* **mensch** *is an* <u>unmensch</u>—*a fine Yiddish word even if it doesn't fly in Scrabble.*)

Oy: an interjection used to express exasperation or pain

Mazeltov: an interjection used to express congratulations, though a closer translation is "good luck"

Schmalz: rendered chicken fat or excessive sentimentality (also **schmaltz**)

My favorite near-Yiddish word in Scrabblish is *schnorkel*, an alternate spelling of *snorkel*. Or perhaps it's snorkeling while **kvetching** about the underwater humidity?

Here are some more Yiddish words that are as good as **gelt** (money):

Bubkes: a tiny amount, virtually nothing (also **bupkes** and **bupkus**) (*literally goat or horse droppings*)

Chatchka: a knickknack (also **chatchke** and **tchotchke**)

Cockamamy: a knickknack, or used to denigrate something as being far-fetched (also **cockamamie**) (*as in, my*

mother: "It's no fun when you play all those **cockamamie** *words!"*)

Dreck: garbage or drivel (also **drek**)

Dreidel: a type of spinning top (also **dreidl**)

Echt: genuine (*It's held by some that the drink "egg cream," which doesn't contain any eggs, derived its name from echt*

Doing It Our Way: "Schlemiel! Schlimazel! Hasenpfeffer Incorporated"

Fans of the old sitcom *Laverne & Shirley* will remember the iconic start to the show's opening theme song, sung while the two young women hop down the Milwaukee block: "**Schlemiel! Schlimazel! Hasenpfeffer** Incorporated." They may have been reciting a Yiddish-American hopscotch chant, but these lyrics could be helpful in another game played upon squares.

Schlemiel: a fool, or someone with bad luck (also **schlemihl**)

Shlimazel: someone perennially unlucky

Hasenpfeffer: a German stew of rabbit or hare

While a shlimazel is likely to fall down a lot, a schlemiel is likely, as the old Yiddish saying goes, "to fall on his back and break his nose."

cream, *the "real" or "genuine" cream drink.*)

Fleishig: describing food containing meat or fat

Ganef: a thief (also **gonef, ganof, gonof, gonoph, gonif,** and **goniff**)

Hutzpa: nerve or gall (also **hutzpah, chutzpa, chutzpah**)

Kibitz: to make small talk, especially as something important is happening nearby (also **kibbitz** and **kibbutz**)

Kvell: to brim with great pride

Kvetch: to complain

Mamzer: a bastard (also **momser**)

Nosh: to snack

Plotz: to become overwhelmed with emotion

Schnook: a fool (also **shnook**)

Schnorrer: a freeloader

Schnoz: the nose, usually a big one (also **schnozz** and **schnozzle**)

Shtetel: a Jewish village (also **shtetl**) (pl. **shtetels, shtetlach**)

Shul: a synagogue (also **schul,** pl. -s or -n)

Tsuris: troubles, worries (also **tsoris, tsorriss,** and **tsores**)

Jeepers Creepers
Interesting Interjections, Exceptional Exclamations, and Outstanding Oaths

The Scrabble board is colorful—why shouldn't its language be colorful too? Although many dirty words have been struck from the *OSPD*, the player who extracts six tiles from the bag and discovers that he's pulled four Is and two Us to add to the V already on his rack does have some recourse; there are many wonderful non-expletive interjections in Scrabblish.

Arriba: used to express excitement

Attaboy: used to cheer a male on

Attagirl: used to cheer a female on

Begorah: a mild oath (*Irish in origin, from "by God!"*) (also

begorra, begorrah)

Bejabers: a mild oath (*likely from "by Jesus!"*)

Bejeezus: a mild oath (*likely from "by Jesus!"*) (also **bejesus**)

Blimy: a mild oath (*primarily British, a contraction of "God blind me"*) (also **blimey**)

Caramba: an exclamation of surprise (*purportedly from the Spanish* carajo, *meaning "penis"*)

Crikey: a mild oath (*likely a euphemism for Christ*) (also **cricky** and **cracky**)

Criminy: a mild oath (*likely a euphemism for Christ, perhaps a contraction of the euphemism "Jiminy Cricket!"*) (also **crimine**)

Cripe: a mild oath (*a euphemism for Christ*) (also **cripes**)

Dammit: a mild oath

Duh: an exclamation of obviousness

Eek: an exclamation of fear

Egad: a mild oath (*likely from "Oh, God"*) (also **egads**)

Faugh: an exclamation of disgust (also **foh**)

Fie: an exclamation of disapproval

Gardyloo: an expression of warning (*from the French* garde à l'eau, *meaning "beware of the water,"* it originated in Scotland and was used to warn pedestrians that one was about to throw dirty water into the street*)

Geez: a mild oath (*a shortened form of Jesus*) (also **jeez**)

Giddyup: used to urge on (also **giddap** and **giddyap**)

Goldarn: an exclamation of anger (also **goldurn**)

Golly: a very mild oath (*perhaps a contraction of "God's body"*)

Gor: a mild oath (*primarily British, a euphemism for God*) (also **gorblimy**)

Gosh: a very mild oath (*a euphemism for God*)

Hey: used to gain attention (also **heigh**)

Hic: expressive of a hiccup (also **huic**)

Hunh: used to ask for something to be repeated or explained

Hup: used to urge on

Jeepers: a mild oath (*a euphemism for Jesus*)

Jiminy: a mild oath (*a euphemism for Jesus*) (also **jimminy**)

Lackaday: an expression of regret (*a contraction of "alack the day"*)

Mm: used to express appreciation or assent

Nertz: an expression of unhappiness (*likely a form of "nuts!"*)

(also **nerts**)

Ochone: an exclamation of lament (*Irish and Scottish, a form of* <u>ohone</u>)

Pah: an exclamation of disgust

Pardi: a mild oath (*Used like "by God." See* Hamlet: *"Ah, ha! Come, some music! come, the recorders! For if the king like not the comedy, Why then, belike, he likes it not, perdy."*) (also **pardee**, **pardie**, **pardy**, **perdie**, and **perdy**)

Pfft: an expression of dismissal, or an expression of a sudden conclusion

Pfui: an expression of dismissal or contempt (also **phooey**)

Phew: an expression of relief

Pht: a mild expression of anger (also **phpht**)

Poh: an expression of disapproval (*I love the* OED*'s definition: "An ejaculation of contemptuous rejection." Accurate bordering on poetic!*) (also **pugh**)

Prithee: an expression used to implore (also **prythee**)

Ptui: an expression of disgust (also **ptooey**)

Quotha: a sarcastic expression used after repeating another's words to imply disbelief, used like "indeed!" (*as in, "Tom played* **ptooey***! 'I knew it because I read it in a book,'* **quotha***!"*)

Rah: used to express encouragement and support in competition

Righto: used to express assent

Shazam: used to express a magical occurrence

Sheesh: an expression of exasperation

Sooey: used as a call to pigs

Touche: used to express a hit in fencing or a good point in conversation

Tsk: an expression of disapproval (also **tsktsk**)

Vive: an expression meaning "long live" (*not to be confused with* **vivers**, *a plural noun for food used mostly in Scotland*)

Voila: used to express something's instantaneous presence

Vum: used to express surprise (*Antiquated, primarily used in New England, this holdover from colonial times comes from* vow, *and was often used in "Well, I vum!" to show surprise.*)

Whamo: used to express an instantaneous, powerful event (also **whammo**)

Whee: used to express enjoyment

Whoa: used to express hesitation

Wirra: used to express sorrow

Wisha: used to express surprise

Yikes: used to express trepidation

Swanny, I Swanny

Swanny, "to declare," is a verb playable only in the first-person singular, as in "I swanny!" Widely unknown outside of the American South, "I swanny" can still be heard there in moments of annoyance or dismay as a very mild oath meaning "I swear," derived from a contraction of "I shall warrant ye." A further shortened form—perhaps the most graceful expression of agitation I've ever heard—is also sometimes heard: "I swan."

Yipe: used to express fear or dismay (also **yipes**)

Yippee: used to express intense happiness

Yoicks: used to encourage hunting dogs

Yum: used to express appreciation for food

Zooks: a mild oath (also **gadzooks,** as well as **godzookery,** -ies) (*a contraction of "God's hooks," referring to Jesus's crucifixion*)

Zounds: a mild oath (*from "God's wounds," referring to Jesus's crucifixion*)

Zowie: an expression of surprise or admiration

Zzz: used to express being asleep

The Answer, My Friend, Is Blowing in the Wind
Plays that Make Scrabble a Breeze

You might be surprised to find what a beeeze it is to make words using these many types of winds found around the world.

In Cuba: Oh, boy, feel that **bayamo blaw.**
In Siberia: **Brr,** what a **bura.**
In Croatia: **Brrr,** what a **bora.**

In France it's a **fon** , in India a **bhut,** in the American
Northwest a **chinook.**
In Switzerland: This is some **bise,** I think I might get a **bleb.**

Bayamo: a strong wind found in Cuba
Blaw: to blow
Brr: used to indicate feeling cold (also **brrr**)
Bura: a violent Eurasian windstorm (also **buran**)
Bora: a cold wind in lowland regions, particularly along the Adriatic
Fon: a warm, dry wind that blows down off some mountains (also
   fohn and **foehn**)
Bhut: a warm dry wind in India (also **bhoot**)
Chinook: a warm wind that flows off the east side of the Rockies; or a
   type of Pacific Northwest salmon named after the Chinook people
Bise: a cold, dry wind, found especially blowing from the northeast in
   Switzerland (also **bize**)
Bleb: a blister

OTHER WINDS

Etesian: a northerly Mediterranean summer wind
Haboob: a violent sandstorm or **duststorm** (*There was something
   of a dustup in Arizona over the use of haboob in local weather reports
   when a storm hit the Phoenix area in July 2011, with some local residents
   complaining that the word could offend American soldiers returning
   from the Middle East.*)
Oe: defined by the *OSPD* as "a whirlwind off the Faeroe Islands," the
   OED's definition is "a small island" (*similar to the words for island in
   Danish, Ø, and Swedish, ö*)
Sarsar: an icy wind (*from the Arabic* çarçar *for a cold wind*)
Simoom: a hot, violent desert wind (also **simoon** and **samiel**)
Williwaw: a violent, cold wind blowing down from a mountain (also
   willyway and **williwau**)

Superhero/Superheroine Secret Identities
Playable Comic Book Heroes and Villains

While proper names are **persona** <u>non</u> <u>grata</u> in Scrabble, some comic book characters are welcome to the board, as they have common noun definitions as well.

Batgirl: a girl whose job it is to mind baseball equipment
Batman: a British officer's orderly
Corsair: a pirate
Hulk: to appear large or intimidating
Iceman: a man whose job it is to supply ice
Ironman: a man of great strength and/or endurance
Joker: one who is habitually making jokes
Magneto: a small electric generator containing a magnet
Mystique: an aura of attractiveness
Riddler: one who poses riddles
Robin: a type of thrush
Superman: an idealized, superior man
Superwoman: from *Merriam-Webster*, "an exceptional woman; *especially*: a woman who succeeds in having a career and raising a family"
Wolverine: a smallish, vicious carnivore of the weasel family, native to the tundra

A Growing Web of Words

The years between the publication of the third *OSPD* in 1996 and the fourth edition eight years later brought with them the explosion of the Internet, which, despite not being a playable word itself, was attended by its own lexicon, including **email**, **ebook**, **webcam**, **webcast**, **blog/weblog** (as a verb and noun), **blogger** (but not weblogger), **firewall**, **login/logon** (but not logout), **metatag**, and **spam/spammer/antispam/spambot**. My two favorites are:

Megaflop: a measure of a computer's calculating speed equal to one million floating point operations ("FLOPS") per second

Wetware: the human brain when considered as functionally equivalent to a computer

Wannabe a Baller?

Some hip-hop terms have made their way into Scrabblish, one way or another:

Baller: "one who balls," according to the *OSPD*

Benjamin: a fragrant gum resin (also **benzoin**)

Biggie: a large person

Doggy: (adj.) similar to a dog, or (n.) a little dog (also **doggie**)

Jiggy: pleasurably excited

Lo: used to call attention

Poppa: father

Skee: to ski

Smalls: pl. of **small** (the small part)

Snoop: to sneakily investigate

Wannabe: a derogatory term for someone who aspires to be like someone else

Put Down a Putdown
Playing with Insults and Casting Aspersions

Scrabble is also a great way to learn a slew of new insults. All of these words are in the *OSPD*, meaning they're considered safe for family play. So dig in and take that **smarty** (an obnoxius know-it-all) you're playing down a peg or two!

SCRABBLISH WAYS TO CALL SOMEONE STUPID

airhead	gomeral (gomerel,	nidget
berk	gomeril)	ninny
birdbrain	gowk	ninnyhammer
bonehead	haverel	saphead
booby	idiot	sawney
butthead	jughead	simp
charlie (charley)	lunk	softhead
chucklehead	lunkhead	spaz
clod	lurdan	staumrel
clodhopper	mome	tomfool
clodpate	mooncalf	
clodpole	moron	
(clodpoll)		
coof		
crackbrain		
cretin		
dobby		
dolt		
dork		
dumbhead		
dumbo		
dummkoff		
dunderhead		
fathead		
feeb		
gaby		

OTHER, MORE-SPECIFIC SCRABBLISH INSULTS

Baddy: a bad person (also **baddie**)

Egghead: one who is overly intellectual

Gomer: a slang term for a hospital patient who the staff feels ought not to be in a hospital (*an acronym for "Get Out of My Emergency Room"*)

Hoser: a sloppy person

Nerd: an unstylish or awkward person (also **nurd**)

Tawpie: a foolish young person, usually a girl

In Scrabblish, there's no aspersion cast upon the **geek**: "a single-minded enthusiast or expert." What a great game!

Should Auld Scots Words Be Forgot?

The *OSPD* is full of Scots words that are useful in the game (**gude**, **hae**, **frae**), but some might ask when these words would ever be useful in real life. Well, come the stroke of midnight next New Year's Eve, you might find yourself once again singing those strange lyrics to Robert Burns's famous poem "Auld Lang Syne." Sure, the drunken revelry makes for a **gude** (good) excuse to slur through the lines, carefree of their meaning, but for the sake of respecting this rather bittersweet poem (if not for the sake of your Scrabble game), let's unpack the title, chorus, and verses using the *OSPD* as a guide.

"Auld Lang Syne" literally means "Old Long Since," or more idiomatically, "Days Gone By," "Old Times," or "(The) Long Time Since."

Here are the lyrics, followed by a translation of the song.

> Should **auld** acquaintance be forgot,
> and never brought to mind?
> Should auld acquaintance be forgot,
> and auld **lang syne**?

CHORUS:
For auld lang syne, my **jo**,
for auld lang syne,
we'll tak a cup o' kindness yet,
for auld lang syne.

And surely ye'll be[1] your pint-**stowp**!
and surely I'll be mine!
And we'll tak a cup o' kindness yet,
for auld lang syne.

We **twa hae** run about the **brae**s,
and pu'd[2] the **gowan**s fine;
But we've wander'd **mony** a weary fit,[3]
sin auld lang syne.

We twa hae paidl'd[4] i' the burn,[5]
Frae morning sun till dine;
But seas between us braid[6] hae roar'd
sin auld lang syne.

And there's a hand, my trusty fiere[7]!
and **gie**'s a hand o' thine!
And we'll tak a right **gude**-willy[8] **waught**,
for auld lang syne.

Definitions of words (as used above) that are either not in the *OSPD* or are used differently in the poem than as defined in the *OSPD*:

1. **be**: to buy

2. pu'd: the past tense of the Scots verb "pou," often written as pu in Burns' time; to "pull" or "pluck"

3. **fit**: foot

4. paidl'd: paddled

5. **burn**: a stream (playable: **burnie**: a brooklet)

6. **braid**: broad

7. fiere: fire (fiere is not playable, but two helpful words are **fierier** and **fieriest**: the comparative and superlative of **fiery** [intensely])

8. gude-willy: goodwill (**willy** is playable as to **willow**: to clean fibers with a certain machine)

Auld: old
Lang: long
Syne: since
Jo: a sweetheart
Stowp: a basin where holy water
   is kept (also **stoup**)
Twa: two
Hae: have
Brae: a hill

Gowan: a daisy or other
   white and yellow flower
Mony: many
Frae: from
Gie: to give
Gude: good
Waught: to drink in deeply,
   to quaff

Righting Your Rack
How to Deal with Unruly Letters

Rack management, the ability to keep a good balance between usable vowels and consonants on one's rack, is one of the most undervalued skills in Scrabble. But sometimes you can't help it—one moment you're okay, and the next vowels or consonants have overtaken your rack like seven children who don't play well with each other.

Don't despair; you have options. The first is swapping these unruly misfits back into the bag for more amenable ones, though sending them back to the cloth orphanage will cost you a turn.

The alternative is to play with what you've got. Luckily, there are more than a few oddball words in the *OSPD* at your disposal for dealing with either too many vowels and too many consonants.

WORDS WITHOUT CONSONANTS

Ae ai, blown by an **oe** oe'r the **eau** to Oahu, said, "**Oi**, look at this **aa**."

Ae: one (adj.)
Ai: a three-toed sloth
Oe: a whirlwind off the Faeroe
   Islands

Eau: water (pl. -x)
Oi: an expression of dismay
   (also **oy**)
Aa: a type of stony, rough lava

FORTY FOUR-LETTER WORDS THAT HAVE THREE VOWELS

Aeon: a long period of time (also **eon**)

Agee: to one side (also **ajee**)

Agio: a surcharge applied when exchanging currency

Ague: sickness associated with malaria

Ajee: to one side (also **agee**)

Akee: a tropical tree

Alae: wings (pl. of **ala**)

Alee: on the side shielded from wind

Amia: a freshwater fish

Amie: a female friend

Anoa: a kind of small buffalo

Awee: a little while

Eaux: waters (pl. of **eau**)

Eide: distinctive appearances of things (pl. of **eidos**)

Emeu: an emu

Etui: an ornamental case

Euro: an Australian marsupial, also known as a **wallaroo**, for being like the kangaroo and wallaby; also a unified currency of much of Europe

Ilea: the terminal portions of small intestines (pl. of **ileum**)

Ilia: pelvic bones (pl. of **ilium**)

Inia: a part of the skull

Ixia: a plant with funnel-shaped flowers

Jiao: a Chinese currency (also **chiao**)

Luau: a large Hawaiian feast

Meou: to meow

Moue: a pouting expression

Naoi: ancient temples (pl. of **naos**)

Obia: a form of sorcery practiced in the Caribbean (also **obeah**)

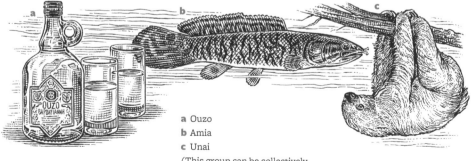

a Ouzo
b Amia
c Unai
(This group can be collectively labeled an "olio.")

Odea: concert halls (pl.
  of **odeum**)
Ogee: an S-shaped molding
Ohia: a Polynesian tree with
  bright flowers (also **lehua**)
Olea: corrosive solutions (pl.
  of **oleum**)
Oleo: margarine
Olio: a miscellaneous collection
Ouzo: Turkish anise-flavored
  liquor
Raia: a non-Muslim Turk
(also **rayah**)
Roue: a lecherous old man
Toea: a currency in Papua
  New Guinea
Unai: a two-toed sloth (pl.
  unau) (*An* **ai** *is a three-toed
  sloth, an* **unai** *is a two-toed
  sloth. That is to say, in the land
  of the sloths the three-toed ai
  is king.*)
Zoea: the larvae of some
  crustaceans

WORDS WITHOUT VOWELS

"**Brr, brrr**, it's cold in this **cwm**," said Carl.

"**Hm, hmm**, it's like negative ten to the **nth**," agreed Hilda.

"**Pst! Psst!** Do you hear someone playing the **crwth**?" asked Carl.

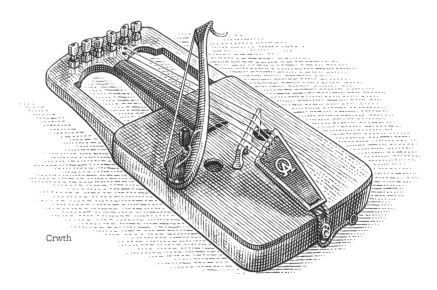

Crwth

> "Playing bop is like Scrabble with all the vowels missing."
>
> —Duke Ellington

"**Sh, shh**!" she said.
"**Mm**," said Carl, "sounds good."
Pfft—the sound disappeared.
"**Pht, phpht**," **tsk**ed Hilda.
Carl **tsktsk**ed too.

Brr: used to indicate that one feels cold (also **brrr**)

Cwm: a cirque (a deep, steep-walled basin on a mountain) (pl. -s) (*pronounced to rhyme with* boom)

Hm: used to express thoughtful consideration (also **hmm**)

Nth: describing an unspecified number of a series

Psst: used to attract someone's attention

Crwth: an ancient stringed instrument (pl. -s)

(*pronounced to rhyme with* booth)

Sh: used to urge silence (also **shh** and **sha**)

Mm: used to express assent or satisfaction

Pfft: used to express a sudden ending

Phpht: used as an expression of mild anger or annoyance (also **pht**)

Tsk: to utter an exclamation of annoyance (-ed, -ing, -s)

Tsktsk: to tsk (-ed, -ing, -s)

The Language of Amour, and Vowels
Words from the French

Growing up, it was always an adventure playing Scrabble with my **pere**, who is **francophone**. His cri **de** coeur of "But it's a word in French!" was common after being informed that—incroyable!—the word he played was not in the *OSPD*. Nevertheless, every once in

Pere: father

Francophone: French-speaking

De: of, from

Jeu: a game (pl. **jeux**)

a while he'd be buoyed by the discovery that a French word he'd attempted was legal in the **jeu**.

Other **mots** (witty remarks) include **frere**, **mere** (a pond, when used as a noun), **ami**, **beau** (**-x**) (a boyfriend), **petit/petite**, **ennui**, **fille**, **femme**, **monsieur**, **bonne** (but not <u>bon</u>), **chez**, **nom**, **sans**, **noir**, **blanche**, **rouge**, **tres**, and **eau** (**-x**). But there's **beaucoup** (also **boocoo** and **bookoo**) more where those came from . . . which is France, I suppose: **Un** (but not <u>deux</u>), **trois**, **quatre** . . . Here are some more:

Artiste: a performance artist
Bastile: a prison (also **bastille**)
Bateau: a type of riverboat (also **batteau**)
Cent: one hundredth of a dollar
Cept: a clan
Chateau: a castle
Comte: to enumerate
Coterie: a tight group
Couteau: a knife
Dauphin: the eldest son of a French king
Dernier: last
Droit: a right
Escargot: an edible snail
Fils: son (pl. fils)
Flic: a French policeman
Frites: French fries
Gateau: a cake
Gauche: devoid of social grace
Gigot: a lamb leg
Jete: a kind of ballet leap
Lycee: a French high school
Matin: a song sung by birds in the morning

Mignon: a small cut of beef
Mille: a thousand
Modiste: one who sells fashionable clothing
Morceau: a short composition
Mouton: a processed sheepskin made to look like that of another animal
Nouveau: of a new style
Pannier: a large container, generally a basket
Pierrot: a sad clown common in French pantomime
Postbourgeois: no longer representative of the middle class
Poutine: French fries covered in cheese curds and gravy (one of the highest-scoring bingos, calorically)
Prochain: next, close to (also **prochein**)
Quartier: a neighborhood or district of a city

Sangfroid: self-possession or "coolness" under pressure

Sieur: an antiquated title of respect for a Frenchman

Tasse: a particular piece of metal armor for the leg (also **tasset**)

Vert: a bright shade of green

And **voila**, now you speak perfect French, and much improved Scrabblish to boot!

The Absolutest Superlatively Weirdest Superlatives & Pluralizations

There are lots of strange words and constructions in the *OSPD*. For instance, if you think you've seen enough of them, and then I give you some more, it's possible that you've seen **enoughs**.

Here are some more of the **mostest** strange: **enows** (**enow**: enough), **uniquer/uniquest**, **cherubims** (**cherubim** is already plural, but maybe you can't get **enow** of a good thing), **absoluter/absolutest**, and **nothings**.

Considering some other unusual plurals is likely to get one thinking deeply about **pluralism** (the coexistence of more than one of a thing) and even **pluralisms**. The names of some centuries—like **duecento** (the thirteenth century), **trecento** (the fourteenth), **seicento** (the seventeenth)—can be pluralized (**duecentos, trecentos,** and **seicentos**). Perhaps it's in those alternative centuries that people played many **tennises**. And while we're **funning** (acting playfully), we can take advantage of the definition of the less common homonym of **none** as one of the seven canonical daily periods of prayer (like vespers, but none takes place at 3 PM and rhymes with *bone*), providing the chance to construct the surprising creation **nones**.

Prefixal

Prefixes and suffixes are supremely important in Scrabble—just imagine your opponent playing **fix** when you held **transes** in your rack. The *OSPD* has pages and pages of words starting with prefixes like *re-* and *un-* and is packed with words that can take suffixes *-er* and *-ing*. Here are some surprising examples:

BEING ALONE

> Bea's **beliquored** brain **bethinks** and **beshrews** her **beblooded** face, before **bepimpled**, now not to be **befingered**, let alone **bekissed**.

Beliquor: to drench in liquor
Bethink: to mull over
Beshrew: to put a curse upon
Beblood: to make bloody
Bepimple: to cover with pimples
Befinger: to touch all over
Bekiss: to kiss all over

OUTING: AN OUTBURST OF OUTBOASTING

> Your throat may **outsnore** mine, your lungs may **outsmoke** mine,
> Your luck may **outjinx** mine, your words may **outkill** mine,
> Your voice may **outhowl** mine, your rage may **outburn** mine,
> You may **outwar** and **outvie** me in almost every way,
> But my **outthrobbing**, **outfawning**, **outpitying** heart **outloves** and **outfeels** yours.

Outing: a short trip, or, **out:** to reveal
Outsnore: to snore more than another does
Outsmoke: to smoke more than another does
Outjinx: to jinx more than another does
Outkill: to kill more than another does

Outhowl: to howl longer or louder than another does
Outburn: to burn longer or stronger than another does
Outwar: to beat another in a war
Outvie: to outdo in competition
Outthrob: to throb more than another
Outfawn: to be more fawning than another
Outpity: to pity more than another does
Outlove: to love more than another does
Outfeel: to feel more than another does

ALSO

Bedunce: to cause to look stupid
Beworm: to infest with worms
Deair: to take air out of
Depeople: to have fewer people at
Disbud: to prune buds from
Disrate: to lower the rating of
Enhalo: to encircle or crown with a halo
Enplane: to board an airplane
Geekdom: the world of geeks
Incommode: to bother
Jibingly: acting in an immovable fashion
Outball: to cry longer or louder than another
Outsmell: to have a better capacity for sensing an odor
 (**outsmelled, outsmelt**)
Overfat: having too much fat (*there is growing attention being paid*
 to the condition of being overfat without being overweight)
Semihobo: a person exhibiting some traits of a hobo
Stewable: capable of being made into a stew
Thingness: the materiality of something
Tubbable: suitable for washing in a bathtub

Some words containing prefixes have surprising definitions:

Bediaper: to decorate with a repeated diamond design
Debride: to surgically remove dead tissue
Outgas: to remove gas from

"Frank, This Is Frank"

The OSPD is home to more **franks** than the Coney Island Nathan's:

> I **ween** the **weeny weenie** costs more **francs** to **frank** than the **weenier weiner**, but the **weeniest wienie**—a **wee wienerwurst**—is so **weensy** it's practically **hotdogging**.

Frank: to mark a piece of mail for free delivery (as an adj.: honest, direct)
Ween: to suppose
Weeny: tiny (**weenier, weeniest**)
Weenie: a hotdog (also **weiner, wienie**)
Franc: a former currency of France
Wee: very little
Wienerwurst: a Vienna sausage or hotdog
Weensy: tiny (**weensier, weensiest**)
Hotdogging: showing off

Words Like They Sound

Fremd: strange, foreign
Furfur: dandruff
Schwa: a particular vowel sound
Smaze: a combination of smog and haze
Zebrass: the offspring of a zebra and an equine, also known as a **zebroid**

"No Nonblondes— What's Going On?"
The Best Non-Words

Nonblonde is not a word, but **nonblack** (a person who is not black) and **nonwhite** (a person who is not white) are. Other notable words starting with non- include: **nongay** (but not nonhetero), **nonself** (foreign material in the body), **nonsked** (an airline that does not have scheduled flights), **nonbook** (a book of little literary merit), and of course there's the golden **nonword**—a word that has no meaning!

These are all much more fun (though of perhaps less help in Scrabble) than **nona**—a strange inclusion in the *OSPD*, which defines the word as "a viral disease," most likely referring to hepatitis C, which is sometimes referred to as "non-A" hepatitis.

Play Some Music
Bands and Musicians That Work in Scrabble

There is a wonderful assortment of playable band or musician names, and the list goes way beyond The **Who** or **Sting**. Sadly, Beatles isn't allowed (although the **fab** four can be found in **beetles**).

> The **abba becks** his sons, a couple of **yardbirds**, to give them some fatherly advice before they head to the bus station down the *backstreet*. "Boys," he says, feeling *eurythmic*, "the **bee gees** and the **garth brooks** no pruners who are **jaggers.** **Aha!** And if a **madonna** overdoes it with the **rem** in the E.R., you let me know! We don't want a **megadeath** on our hands." "**Wilco**," they reply, "just remember to feed the **feist**."

Play It Again, Sam: Musical Notes

The diatonic musical scale: **do**, **re**, **mi**, **fa**, **sol**, **la**, **ti**.

Do: the first tone of the diatonic musical scale (pl. **dos**)

Re: the second tone of the diatonic musical scale

Mi: the third tone of the diatonic musical scale

Fa: the fourth tone of the diatonic musical scale

Sol: the fifth tone of the diatonic scale (also **so**, pl. **sos**)

La: the sixth tone of the diatonic scale

Ti: the seventh tone of the diatonic scale (also **si**, pl. **sis**)

Abba: father
Beck: to beckon
Yardbird: an army recruit
Backstreet: a minor street
Eurythmic: in a generally upbeat, positive mood (also **eurhythmic**)
Bee: a type of flying insect
Gee: to move to the right
Garth: a garden or yard
Brook: to tolerate or permit
Jagger: one who cuts unevenly
Aha: an expression of surprise, triumph, or conclusion
Madonna: a former title of respect for a woman in Italy
Rem: a dosage of ionizing radiation
Megadeath: a unit of measure equal to one million human casualites (*the band's name is spelled Megadeth*)
Wilco: used to express consent, particularly over radio transmissions, like "roger" (*from "will comply"*)
Feist: a small hunting dog

Performance-Enhancing Drugs
Or This Is Your Board;
This Is Your Board ... on Drugs

Performance-enhancing drugs aren't a problem with word games, though as in other arenas, some competitive players adhere to regimens of varieties of pills and supplements. While the jury is out on just how much good most drugs do for a player's game, it's safe to say that simply knowing the names of a lot drugs and drug-related words is a simpler—let alone cheaper and more interesting—way to up your game. Here are some good ones to start with, just for a little taste.

Bedrug: to make sleepy through drugs
Benny: an amphetamine tablet (from <u>Benzedrine</u>)
Bhang: the hemp plant in India
Bidi: a cigarette of India (also **beedi**)
Bogart: to use without sharing (*From Humphrey Bogart's habit of keeping a cigarette dangling in his mouth, even while speaking. Try it with a blank during your next game: it's healthier, and more intimidating.*)
Charas: hashish
Cig: a cigarette
Dagga: Indian marijuana
Dex: a sulfate used as a stimulant (**dexie:** a tablet thereof)
Doobie: a marijuana cigarette
Druggy: affected by drugs (**druggie:** a drug addict [pl. -s])
Ganja: cannabis used for smoking (also **ganjah**)
Gasper: a cigarette (*chiefly British*)
Hashhead: one who smokes a lot of hashish
Hashish: a cannabis-based narcotic
Joypop: to use habit-forming drugs
Junkie: one addicted to drugs (**junky** *is defined as "worthless"*)
Kahuna: a Hawaiian shaman

Kef: hemp smoked to euphoria (also **kif, kaif, keef, kief**) (*from the Arabic* kayf, *meaning well-being or pleasure*)

Lude: a tablet of methaqualone

Maryjane: marijuana

Meth: methamphetamine

Narc: an undercover drug agent (also **narco**) (**nark** is the verb)

Pothead: one who smokes marijuana

Qat: the leaf of a type of shrub, chewed or used in tea as a mild stimulant (also *kat khat*)

Roofie: a tablet of a powerful benzodiazepine sedative

Scag: heroin (also **skag**)

Spliff: a marijuana cigarette

Stoner: one who pelts another with stones (also known as **lapidating**)

Toke: to take a drag of a marijuana cigarette (*one who does this is a* **toker**)

Trank: a drug that tranquilizes (also **tranq**)

Trippy: suggestive of the experience of being on psychedelic drugs

DDDEEE and IMNNNUUUU Is All I Want to Say to You

Deeded is the only Scrabblish word that uses two letters three times each.

Unununium is the only word in Scrabblish that begins with the same pair of letters three times in a row. It's the former name of the element roentgenium—which, for a reason I cannot discern, is not playable. The name unununium came from the element's atomic number of 111. Before it was christened roentgenium (Rg), *unununium* had probably the coolest symbol on the periodic table: Uuu.

A, B, C, D, E, F, Blank

There's no playable word using just the first seven letters of the alphabet, *a* through *g* (may I humbly propose the supremely elegant cafbdge?). But there are two playable (and common) eight-letter words that can be made using all of the letters *a* through *f*, plus two blanks. Can you think of them?

Answer: **boldface** and **feedback**

Complete List of All 101 Acceptable Two-Letter Words

1. **Aa:** a type of stony, rough lava (*There are 16 two-letter words starting with* a, *so you have a 62-percent chance that any tile you put after an A will make a word.*)
2. **Ab:** an abdominal muscle
3. **Ad:** an advertisement
4. **Ae:** one (adj.)
5. **Ag:** agriculture
6. **Ah:** an exclamation
7. **Ai:** a three-toed sloth
8. **Al:** a type of East Indian tree
9. **Am:** the first-person singular present form of "to be"
10. **An:** indefinite article
11. **Ar:** the letter *r*
12. **As:** similar to
13. **At:** in the position of
14. **Aw:** an expression of protest or sadness
15. **Ax:** a sharp-edged tool
16. **Ay:** a vote in the affirmative
17. **Ba:** the soul in ancient Egyptian spirituality
18. **Be:** to exist
19. **Bi:** a bisexual
20. **Bo:** a pal
21. **By:** a side issue
22. **De:** of; from
23. **Do:** a tone of the scale
24. **Ed:** education
25. **Ef:** the letter *f*
26. **Eh:** used to express doubt
27. **El:** an elevated train
28. **Em:** the letter *m*
29. **En:** the letter *n*
30. **Er:** used to express hesitation
31. **Es:** the letter *s*
32. **Et:** a past tense of *eat*
33. **Ex:** the letter *x*
34. **Fa:** a tone of the diatonic scale

35. **Fe:** a Hebrew letter
36. **Go:** a Japanese board game sometimes known as Othello (-s)
37. **Ha:** used to express surprise
38. **He:** a pronoun signifying a male
39. **Hi:** an expression of greeting
40. **Hm:** used to express consideration
41. **Ho:** used to express surprise
42. **Id:** the least censored part of the three-part psyche
43. **If:** a possibility
44. **In:** to harvest (*yes, a verb in Scrabblish; takes* -s, -ed, -ing)
45. **Is:** the third-person singular present form of "to be"
46. **It:** a neuter pronoun
47. **Jo:** a sweetheart
48. **Ka:** the spiritual self in ancient Egyptian spirituality
49. **Ki:** the vital life force in Chinese spirituality (also **qi**)
50. **La:** a tone of the diatonic scale
51. **Li:** a Chinese unit of distance
52. **Lo:** an expression of surprise
53. **Ma:** mother
54. **Me:** a singular objective pronoun
55. **Mi:** a tone of the diatonic scale (M *is the loosest consonant. In the first position, it'll pair up with every vowel, plus* y [*ma, me, mi, mo, mu, my*].

In the second position, it'll pair up with any vowel except i [*am, em, om, um*]. *It'll even pair up with hm. And if it can't find anyone else, it can even pair with itself:* **mm***!*)

56. **Mm:** an expression of assent
57. **Mo:** a moment
58. **Mu:** a Greek letter
59. **My:** a first-person possessive adjective
60. **Na:** no; not
61. **Ne:** born with the name of
62. **No:** a negative answer
63. **Nu:** a Greek letter
64. **Od:** a hypothetical force
65. **Oe:** a whirlwind off the Faeroe Islands
66. **Of:** originating from
67. **Oh:** an exclamation of surprise
68. **Oi:** an expression of dismay (also **oy**)
69. **Om:** a sound used as a mantra
70. **On:** the batsman's side in cricket
71. **Op:** a style of abstract art dealing with optics
72. **Or:** the heraldic color gold (*a noun, so pl.* -s)
73. **Os:** a bone
74. **Ow:** used to express pain
75. **Ox:** a clumsy person
76. **Oy:** an expression of dismay (also **oi**)

a Os
b Ai
c Za
d Ax
e Xu
f Oe

77. **Pa:** a father
78. **Pe:** a Hebrew letter
79. **Pi:** a Greek letter
80. **Qi:** the central life force in traditional Chinese culture (also **ki**)
81. **Re:** a tone of the diatonic scale
82. **Sh:** used to encourage silence
83. **Si:** a tone of the diatonic scale (also **ti**)
84. **So:** a tone of the diatonic scale (also **sol**)
85. **Ta:** an expression of thanks
86. **Ti:** a tone of the diatonic scale
87. **To:** in the direction of
88. **Uh:** used to express hesitation
89. **Um:** used to express hesitation
90. **Un:** one
91. **Up:** to raise (-s, -ped, -ping)
92. **Us:** a plural pronoun
93. **Ut:** the musical tone C in the French solmization system, now replaced by **do**
94. **We:** a first-person plural pronoun
95. **Wo:** woe
96. **Xi:** a Greek letter
97. **Xu:** a monetary unit of Vietnam equal to one-hundredth of a dong (also **sau** pl. **xu**)
98. **Ya:** you
99. **Ye:** you
100. **Yo:** an expression used to attract attention
101. **Za:** a pizza

The Land of Za

The word **za** (as in, "I'll have a slice of za" or "Let's go for some za") became popular on Southern California college campuses in the 1970s. These days there's a fairly well-known pizza place in San Francisco called Za's, but the word has never quite caught on on the East Coast, where—outside of Scrabble—it's just as likely to hear a slice of toast referred to as "toe."

The Baddest Definition
in the *OSPD*

Bad is probably one of the best entries in the *OSPD*. It has three definitions:

Bad: (adj. **worse, worst**) not good in any way
Bad: (n. -s) something that is bad
Bad: (adj. **badder, baddest**) very good
     So on second thought, it's probably one of the **baddest** entries.

Badass isn't an acceptable word, but one may play **bagass**, an alternative spelling of **bagasse**, crushed sugarcane.

Words Gone Wild
The Surprising Side of Many Boring Nouns

Definitions in the *OSPD* (as well as this book) are often chosen to highlight uncommon usage. The idea is that words one would generally think of in one way (**clock**: an instrument that displays the time) may also be used differently (to time with a stopwatch). Providing the definitions of these words as verbs signals their capacity to take on suffixes like -*ed* and -*ing*, in addition to the -*s* that can be tagged onto most nouns and verbs.

     While the *OSPD* contains oodles of nouns that one could readily conceive of as verbs (**fish**: to try to catch fish; **flower**: to bloom), it also includes many stranger entries:

Beetle: to stick out or project
Belly: to swell outward
Bib: to drink alcohol
Brute: to shape a diamond by rubbing it with another diamond

a Candle
b Disk
c Pink

Candle: to examine eggs for freshness in front of a light

Cat: to hoist an anchor to the cathead

Cheese: to stop

Chess: to weed

Coke: to distill coal in order to create carbon fuel

Crepe: to frizz or spread out hair, particularly fake hair used by actors

Disk: to break up land, as with a hoe or plow

Fig: to adorn or dress up

Fruit: to come to bear fruit

Guy: to make fun of (*after the British villain/conspirator Guy Fawkes*)

Hip: to construct a roof

Hull: to remove a dry shell or covering from a fruit, nut, or seed

In: to harvest

Iris: to make to look like a rainbow (*from Iris, the divine messenger in Greek mythology, who took the form of the rainbow and acted as messenger between the gods and humans*)

Kite: to use a check to obtain money fraudulently, to prey on another (*after the kite, a bird of prey similar to an eagle*)

Lamp: to look at or observe

Lens: to film something

Low: to make a sound like that of cattle

May: to gather flowers in the springtime

Maze: to bewilder

Necklace: to lynch by placing a tire around the neck and setting it on fire

Pancake: to land an airplane by having it drop vertically for several feet

Peach: to inform against another (*as in* impeach)

Pink: to cut a saw-toothed edge into cloth

Quail: to cower

Rug: to tear roughly

Shark: to live by trickery

Style: to name or make in a fashion

Super: to reinforce a book's spine with thin cotton mesh

Toilet: to wash, dress, and attend to one's appearance (*from the French* toilette, *which first referred to a thin cloth doily that covered the clothes during shaving or hairdressing*)

Tomcat: to act in a sexually promiscuous way—used of a male

Weird: (n.) one's destiny (Scottish); (v.) to cause to feel odd; (adj.) mysteriously strange (*from the Old English* wyrd, *meaning "fate;" as* **dree** *means "to endure," one can be told to "Dree your weird," or endure your fate.*)

And then there are words you might not expect to see as nouns:

The **bigs** bring **go** to the **stank**.

Big: one of great importance

Go: a Japanese board game

Stank: a pond

Ironically, **bingo**, which is often used as a verb by Scrabble players, as in "She <u>bingoed</u> three times **agin** (against) me!" is not listed as a verb in the *OSPD*.

Little Words for Lazy People

They say that sloth is one of the seven deadly sins. Well, here's a short list of short words to make your game a little deadlier, too. These are particularly well suited for play while still in bed at noon on a Sunday.

Jauk: to dawdle
Laze: to lounge idly
Loll: to lounge idly
Moon: to spend time idly dreaming (*usually used with "away"*)
Sweer: lazy or disinclined to act
Toit: to move about lazily
Veg: to spend time idly

Please Play with the Animals

Aoudad: a type of wild sheep also known as Barbary sheep
Aasvogel: a vulture (*from the Afrikaans* <u>aas</u>, *meaning "carrion," and* <u>vogel</u>, *meaning "bird"*)
Biddy: a hen
Bombyx: a silkworm
Booklice: insects—though technically not lice—that damage books
Bossy: a calf or cow, or (adj.) domineering
Cero: a type of mackerel
Cimex: a bedbug
Coypu: a large river rat, also known as a **nutria**
Cuscus: a type of possum
Dabchick: a small water bird also known as the little *grebe* (*Dabchick is the only word in the* OSPD *that contains the letter combination* abc.)
Dhole: a type of wild dog found in India
Dikdik: a type of small antelope
Drongo: a tropical bird (*The bird is known for its unusual behavior, which may be why in Australia* drongo *is an insult something like "idiot."*)
Ebbet: a green newt also known as a spring peeper

a Aasvogel   f Drongo
b Teiid   g Wapiti
c Kinkajou   h Poyou
d Ged   i Zyzzyva
e Coypu   j Numbat

Egger: a kind of moth known for its tentlike webs

Firebrat: a small, wingless insect similar to the silverfish

Ged: a pike

Godwit: a large wading bird

Hogg: a young sheep, from about nine to eighteen months, until its second tooth comes in

Hyrax: a small harelike mammal

Kinkajou: an arboreal mammal also known as the honey bear, occasionally kept as a pet

Numbat: a small, endangered Australian marsupial

Okapi: an African mammal resembling the zebra, but more closely related to the giraffe

Oldsquaw: the long-tailed duck (*Long-tailed duck is the preferred name and growing in usage on account of the offensive nature of* squaw.)

Oldwife: a marine fish found in the Indian and Pacific oceans (*Its name is derived from the sound it makes grinding its teeth when caught.*)

Opah: a marine fish also known as a **moonfish**, **cusk**, or **torsk**

Oquassa: a small freshwater trout

Oxpecker: a starling found in Africa

Pard: a leopard (**pardine:** pertaining to a leopard) (*The word* leopard *is actually a Greek compound of* leon *for lion and* pardos *for male panther, as leopards were thought to be part lion and part panther.*)

Pekepoo: a dog that is a cross between a Pekingese and a poodle (also **peekapoo**)

Pika: a small mammal like a rabbit

Platy: a small tropical fish, also known as platyfish (also [adj.] split into thin, flat pieces)

Pogy: a marine fish of the herring family

Pollywog: a tadpole (also **polliwog**)

Potto: a lemur of tropical Africa—sometimes called a softly-softly

Poyou: an armadillo found in Argentina

Puli: a type of sheepdog (-lis, -lik), (also pl. of **pul:** a coin of Afghanistan [-s, -i])

Punkie: a biting gnat

Quinnat: a chinook salmon

Rhebok: a species of African antelope (*The Africaans/Dutch spelling is* <u>Reebok</u>, *and was chosen as the name of the sneaker company from*

a South African dictionary won in a race by one of the grandsons of the company's founder.)

Sajou: a long-tailed monkey also known as a capuchin (also **sapajou**)

Skua: any of several predatory seabirds

Spitz: a type of dog having a heavy coat, such as the Pomeranian

Squab: a young or baby pigeon

Squilla: any of various burrowing crustaceans with movable, stalked eyes

Starnose: a mole with a large, twenty-two-tentacled, starlike nose

Tahr: an Asian goatlike mammal

Teiid: a tropical American lizard also known as the whiptail

Veery: a small songbird

Vizslal: a Hungarian dog known for its blend of hunting skills and domesticity

Volvox: a green algae

Wapiti: elk

Whaup: a European bird

Whippet: a small, swift dog similar to the greyhound

Xerus: an African ground squirrel

Yapok: the water opossum (also **yapock**)

Zander: a freshwater fish like perch

Zoril: a small African weasel (also **zorilla**, **zorrille**, **zorillo**)

Zyzzyva: a tropical weevil (*Though the penultimate word in the OSPD,* **zyzzyva** *is often the last word listed in dictionaries. As such, it's often used metaphorically to mean the last word on a subject. It has also been the answer to clues in at least three* New York Times *crossword puzzles—unsurprisingly on two Fridays and a Saturday, days of notoriously difficult puzzles.*)

Say It Ain't Sos
Bad Grammar, Good Words

Barefit: without socks or shoes

Brung: a past tense of brought

Dandriff: dandruff

Deers: plural of deer

Drownd: to drown (*This is present tense; past tense of* **drownd** *is* **drownded**. *Remember Paulie's reaction in* Rocky IV *when little Rocky Jr. sprays him with* **whipt** *cream?*)

Git: to get

Irregardless: regardless

Purty: pretty

Rin: to run

Strucken: struck

Wimmin and **Womyn:** woman (*erroneously left out of some editions of* OSPD, *but legal*)

PLAYING WITHOUT PIZZAZZ

Although it was accidentally left out of some initial printings, **pizzazz** is now included in the OSPD, along with **pizzazzy** and **pizzazzes**, though with their four **izzards** (the letter *z*), none of the words is playable with Scrabble's single Z and two blanks.

However, they are all possible in Super Scrabble, which enlarges the Scrabble board size from 225 squares to 441 and doubles the number of tiles from 100 to 200. Though the tile distribution in Super Scrabble does not simply double the distribution of classic Scrabble, it does provide two Zs and two blanks, making the three words possible.

Knickknack is another interesting case. With four Ks, it too is impossible to play in standard Scrabble. Its length (more than eight letters) necessarily keeps it out of the OSPD. It was erroneously excluded from the OWL but is playable—if only you can manage it.

Kickback would require both blanks, the K, and both Cs. But if you're set on playing a three-K word at some point, try to serve up the marvelous **krumkake**, the thin Norwegian waffle cookie popular in the American Midwest.

CATCH SOME Zs

Besides **pizzazz**, **pizzazzes**, and **pizzazzy**, there are a surprising number of words—ten!—that require the use of the Z plus both blanks used as Zs. They say there's a season for everything; I'm not sure when the season to play a Z with two blanks is, except I suppose, if the opportunity arises to play **zzz** or **zzzyzva**, no matter what the situation, one has to take it, just 'cause, **coz** (cousin.)

Bezazz: pizazz
Pazazz: pizazz
Pizazz: the quality of being excited (-es)
Pizazzy: having pizazz
Pizzaz: pizazz
Zizzle: to sizzle (-d, -s)
Zyzzyva: a tropical weevil
Zzz: used to suggest the sound of sleeping

There are no words that use more than one Q.

Words that take two Xs are **maxixe** (a Brazilian dance, pl. -s) and **paxwax** (a nuchal ligament of a quadruped, pl. -es). (Not to be confused with the old way to purchase baseball cards, wax packs.)

Bathroom Breaks
Making It "Jake" to
Use the "Jakes"

Competitive Scrabble games typically afford players a total of 25 minutes for each player to play. One problem with timed play is, as Annie Warbucks famously put it, "When you gotta go, you gotta go." In today's tournaments, a player can get up to use the **pissoir** (urinal) in the **lav** (bathroom) or make a **caca** (excrement) in the **john** (toilet), and the clock ticks away from that allotted 25 minutes during the player's absence at the **potty** (toilet). Not so in competitive Scrabble's early days.

In New York chess clubs in the 1970s, instead of 25 total minutes to use over the course of the game, players had 3 minutes to make each move.

If a player failed to play in 3 minutes, the turn was forfeited—and the player was you-know-what out of luck. Accordingly, if a player left the board to make a **doodoo** (feces), the clock ticked away. An extended absence from the table could cost a player several moves in a row, and during that time the opponent could go ahead and play after each forfeiture. A helpful rule of thumb for tournament players: if you must **weewee** (to urinate), do it in a **wee** (short period of time).

Three other useful five-letter words from the **privy** (outhouse) one should be privy to are **biffy** (a toilet), **gleet** (to discharge mucus from the urethra, often associated with gonorrhea), and **gripy** (causing sharp pains in the bowels).

Tan Tiles, Silver Screen

The 2004 documentary *Word Wars* is an entertaining and evocative look at professional Scrabble playing, but plenty of other movies also offer important Scrabble tips. The following titles from the **cinematiques** (a film archive where old films are screened) are all playable: *terminator* (one who ends something), *transformers* (instruments for changing an electrical current), *jurassic* [**park**] (very old), **moonstruck** (overcome with romantic feelings), *synecdoche*, **goldeneye** (a species of duck), **dumbo** (a stupid person), and **fantasia** (a type of free-form musical composition).

Shrek isn't playable, but **schrick** (a fright) is. And there was that Judy Holliday/Jack London feature with Kim Novack called *Phffft!* If only it was **Pfft**! or **Pht**! or **Phpht**! it would've worked.

The Three Saddest Words in Scrabble ...

Climaxless: devoid of a climax
Poetless: devoid of a poet
Wineless: devoid of wine

Depending on your tastes, you may also decry the states of being **weedless** and **pipeless**, though the citizens of Margaritaville might lament being **limeless** even more.

... And Some of the Funnest

"Eating that **funest fugu** was **funner** than the **funnest funfest**, it was like a **funplex** in a **funfair**" said the **fubsy funnyman.**

Funest: portending evil or death

Fugu: the puffer fish, known for its toxicity to humans if not properly prepared (*This is the Japanese name for the fish.*)

Fun: amusing (**funner, funnest**), also to act in a playful manner (**funs, funned, funning**)

Funfest: a party

Funplex: a building in which to play games

Funfair: an amusement park

Fubsy: chubby and squat

Funnyman: a comedian

Cheers!
Ways to Drink, What to Drink, and What You Are When You've Drunk Too Much

WAYS TO DRINK

To pour: **skink**

To drink a little: **bib, dram**

To drink to the health of someone: **wassail**

To drink too much: **tope, swizzle, chugalug**

WHAT TO DRINK

Wines and champagnes: **zin**, **brut**, **fino**, **cuvee**, **vino**, **glogg**, **macon**, **mirin**, **negus**, **perry**, **rioja**, **soave**, **tokay**

Cocktails and Spirits: **kir**, **arak** (**arrack**), **grog**, **nogg**, **ouzo**, **raki**, **sloe**, **hooch** (**hootch**), **pisco**, **tafia** (a cheap rum)

Beers: **kvass** (**kvass**, **quass**) (a Russian beer made of fermented rye bread)

Other: **kumys** (**koumis**, **koumiss**, **koumyss**, **kumiss**) (*However one spells* **kumys***, it's strange to most Americans' taste, as this Mongolian beverage consists of fermented horse milk.*)

"To Good Letters!": Toasts in Scrabble

Lehayim: a traditional Jewish toast (-s) (also **lechayim**)

Prosit: an expression used in toasting (also **prost**) (*from the Latin* prosit, *meaning "may it be good"*)

Slainte: used as a toast in Ireland, meaning "to health"

Skoal: to toast one's health in Scandanavia (*referring to the drinking vessel—literally "bowl"*)

WHEN YOU'VE DRUNK TOO MUCH

Ways to be drunk: **fou, blotto, beery** (that is, on booze), **boozy, stinko, tiddly** (that is, just a little), **sozzled, squiffed** (**squiffy**), **swacked**, having **jimjams** (violent delirium)

General drunkards: **sot, alky, wino, dipso, shicker, boozer, tosspot**

Specialized drunkards: **ginny** (drunk on gin), **rubby** (one who gets drunk on rubbing alcohol), **stewbum** (a drunken bum)

The Phiz and the Bod

Auris: the ear (pl. **aures**)

Bazoo: the mouth

Beezer: the nose

Bod: body

Buccal: regarding the cheek

Coxa: the hip (pl. **coxae**, adj. **coxal**)

Craw: the stomach

Derm: the skin (also **derma**)

Dorsum: the back

Eyne: a plural of eye (also **eyen**)

Glim: a light or lamp, or an eye

Glossa: the tongue

Haeffet: the cheekbone and temple

Jole: the jowl

Jugal: regarding the cheekbone

Kyte: the stomach

Lingua: the tongue

Loof: the palm of the hand

Medius: the middle finger (pl. **medii**)

Nates: (n./pl.) the buttocks

Neif: the fist or hand (also **nieve**)

Nevus: a birthmark

Nucha: the nape of the neck

Omer: a bone in the skull

Orad: toward the mouth

Petto: the breast

Phiz: the face (*a shortening of* **physiognomy**)

Risus: a grin

Sudor: sweat

Wame: the belly

Wizzen: the throat (also **weasand**)

And Bingo Was His Name-o

A *bingo* is the North American term for playing all seven letters on one rack in one turn. A bonus of 50 points is awarded for a bingo. (In the United Kingdom, playing all seven letters is more often referred to as a "bonus.")

There are about 50,000 possible seven-letter bingos in Scrabble, plus all the words longer than seven letters that can be made using tiles already on the board. While it would be great to know them all, don't feel too bad if you don't think you're up to the task. U.S., Canadian, and World Scrabble champion Joel Watnick owns up to (only!) having memorized about 16,000 of them.

Let's **lour** (lower) our sights a little, and have a look at some of the more useful and interesting bingos out there and how to play them.

SCORING BIG BY PLAYING THE ODDS

Of the 3,199,724 different combinations of seven letters you can draw for your first rack, the good news is that you have only about a 1 in 800,000 shot at getting stuck with seven of the same letter. (It would have to be all As, Es, Is, or Os, as those are the only tiles of which there are at least seven.)

In *Word Freak*, Stefan Fatsis reports that the chances of choosing letters that could form a playable bingo with that first draw are 12.63 percent, or just over 1 in 8. The odds of spotting that bingo, of course, are another story.

The least likely opening rack one might draw is BBJKQXZ, whereby the B could be replaced by any tile of which there are two in the bag (B, C, F, H, M, P, V, W, Y, and the blanks). But the odds come in at around 16 billion to 1, so you may want to hold on to this as interesting trivia, rather than hold your breath in hopes of not drawing such a crummy **septet** (group of seven).

THE MOST LIKELY DRAW

The most likely seven letters one might draw to open the game are AEINORT. At first glance, this may seem like meaningless trivia. The odds aren't great (at about 1 in 9,530), and, worse still, the rack doesn't offer any seven-letter bingos. But if you draw these letters and are set to play first, the best thing to do is actually to pass. As it happens, if your opponent plays any of twelve different letters (A, B, C, D, H, L, N, P, R, S, T, or Z), you've got a bingo waiting for you. If he plays a T, you have the chance to play **tentoria** (the internal skeletal form of an insect's head—*what an awesome word!*). Here's a list of other ways you can bingo by passing your first turn, if any of these letters are played while you are holding AEINORT:

A   **Aeration:** the act of supplying with air
B   **Baritone:** a deep, male voice
       Obtainer: one who takes possession
       Reobtain: to retake possession
       Taborine: a **taboret:** a small drum
C   **Actioner:** an action film
       Anoretic: an anorexic
       Creation: something made
       Reaction: a response
D   **Arointed:** past tense of **aroint:** to order away (*as from* Macbeth: "*Aroint thee, witch!*")
       Ordinate: a geographic position
       Rationed: past tense of **ration:** to allow or distribute a fixed amount
H   **Antihero:** an ignoble protagonist
L   **Oriental:** "an inhabitant of an eastern country," according to the *OSPD*
       Relation: a connection between multiple things
N   **Anointer:** one who ritually applies a substance
       Reanoint: to reapply a substance as part of a ritual
P   **Atropine:** a substance used to dilate the pupil
R   **Anterior:** toward the front
S   **Notaries:** plural of **notary:** a type of public official who deals with legal documents
       Senorita: an unmarried Spanish woman or girl
T   **Tentoria:** (n./pl.) the internal skeletal form of an insect's head
Z   **Notarize:** to have a notary certify a document

MAKE EACH OF YOUR RETINAE A TRAINEE FOR THESE BINGOS

The most likely seven letters one can draw that create a seven-letter bingo to start the game are AEEINRT, which can create **retinae** (the plural of **retina, retinas** is another **pluralization**) and **trainee**.

Odds are still slim (just 1 in 14,000), but the chances of seeing this combination sometime during a game, especially as players gain control over their racks and their ability to get rid of unhelpful letters by dumping them or trading them in, increase dramatically.

FOUR WORDS IT NEVER MAKES SENSE TO PLAY

One word one should (almost) never ever play is **tisane** (an herbal tea, also **ptisan**). Say it three times: **tisane tisane tisane**. It's insane to play **tisane**. Remember it. Now forget about using it.

Likewise for its anagrams—**seitan** (wheat gluten), **tenias** (tapeworms), and **tineas** (fungal skin diseases like ringworm)—don't play these either. (Many players remember this stem as <u>satine</u> or <u>anties</u>, but considering how gross **tenias** and **tineas** are, maybe it's those words that are easier to remember not to play.)

The reason is that **tisane** is the most malleable six-letter combination in Scrabble. It's capable of creating bingos with every letter except *j*, *q*, and *y*, for a total of sixty-nine different words. Except in the most extreme circumstances (there are no more letters in the bag, or you feel you must block an opportunity for your opponent to play a high-scoring bingo, or there's absolutely no place on the board that could create a possibility for you to place a bingo, etc.), there's no reason to play those six letters.

Do your future opponents a disfavor and at least become passingly familiar with this list. If you see the letters TISANE on your rack, start shaking your head until the bingo falls out of your ear (or a tenia does). Then stick it on the board and collect your 50 bonus points. Then find me and buy me a beer.

TISANE plus:

A   **Entasia:** a muscle spasm

    Taenias: a headband or ribbon worn in ancient Greece (*a genus of tapeworms takes its name from it*)

B   **Banties:** plural of **banty:** a small type of poultry (also **bantam,** *which gives its name to* ***bantamweight*** *fighters*)

    Basinet: a medieval open-faced helmet

C   **Acetins:** plural of **acetin:** a liquid acetate

    Cineast: a film enthusiast

D   **Destain:** to eliminate a stain

    Detains: plural of **detain:** to prevent from leaving

    Instead: in place of

    Nidates: present tense of **nidate:** to become implanted in the uterus

    Sainted: past tense of **saint:** to canonize into sainthood

    Stained: past tense of **stain:** to soil with a lasting mark

E   **Etesian:** a northerly Mediterranean summer wind

F   **Fainest:** superlative form of **fain:** happily (*as in Juliet to Romeo:* "*Fain would I dwell on form. Fain, fain deny / What I have spoke. But farewell compliment! / Dost thou love me?*")

G   **Easting:** a distance traveled eastwardly

    Eatings: plural of **eating**

    Ingates: plural of **ingate:** an entrance, particularly for molten metal to enter a mold

    Ingesta: ingested material, particularly orally

    Seating: seat cushion upholstery

    Teasing: present participle of **tease:** to mock, annoy, or toy with

H   **Sheitan:** the devil or an evil spirit in Islam (also **shaitan**) (*similar in origin and meaning to Satan*)

    Sthenia: unusually great strength or energy (*from the Greek word from strength, sthenos, from which the English term is also derived*)

I   **Isatine:** a chemical compound used to make a synthetic indigo dye (also **isatin**)

K   **Intakes:** plural of **intake:** the process of taking in or absorbing

L   **Elastin:** a protein found in connective tissue

Entails: present tense of **entail:** to limit an inheritance to specific heirs

Nailset: a tool in home construction for driving nails

Salient: a part of a battlefield front that projects into enemy territory

Saltine: a salted cracker, also known as a soda cracker

Slainte: used as a toast in Ireland, meaning "to health"

Tenails: plural of **tenail:** an exterior defense standing in front of a fortress (also **tennaille**)

M **Etamins:** plural of **etamine:** a soft cotton fabric (also **etamines**)

Inmates: plural of **inmate:** a prisoner in a jail

Tameins: plural of **tamein:** a skirt worn by Burmese women

N **Inanest:** superlative of **inane:** silly, devoid of reason

Stanine: one of nine sets into which standardized test scores are divided

O **Atonies:** plural of **atony:** a lack of muscular strength

P **Panties:** plural of **pantie:** a woman's or girl's undergarment (also **panty**)

Patines: present tense of **patine:** to apply a patina

Sapient: a wise person, a sage (*as in* King Lear, *when he addresses the Fool: "Thou sapient, sir, sit here!"*)

Spinate: having thorns or spines

R This seven-letter combination is the most prodigious in Scrabble, creating 9 seven-letter bingos, as well as being the basis for 78 eight-letter bingos and about 250 nine-letter bingos.

Anestri: plural of **anestrus:** a period of sexual dormancy in cyclically breeding mammals

Antsier: comparative of **antsy:** nervous, restless

Nastier: comparative of **nasty:** mean, wicked

Ratines: plural of **ratine:** a rough fabric that is loosely woven

Retains: present tense of **retain:** to continue to possess

Retinas: plural of **retina:** a light-sensative membrane of the eye

Retsina: a Greek wine

Stainer: one who stains

Stearin: a triglyceride used to make candles and soap

a Nailset
b Basinet
c Retinas
d Panties

e Spinate
f Saltine
g Tisane

S **Entasis:** a curve applied to architectural surfaces, particularly columns

Nasties: plural of **nasty:** something nasty

Seitans: plural of **seitan:** wheat gluten

Sestina: a particular type of 39-line poem composed of six **sextains** (a six-line stanza) and one **tercet** (a three-line stanza) in which the last words of the first sextain are used in a particular order to end every line for the length of the poem

Tansies: plural of **tansy:** an herb with a yellow flower, also known as **mugwort**

Tisanes: plural of **tisane:** an herbal tea (also **ptisan**) (*You have the author's blessing to use* **tisanes** *in the plural.*)

T **Instate:** to put into office

Satinet: a thin satin fabric

U **Aunties:** plural of **aunty:** an aunt (**aunties** *is one of the cutest bingos out there*)

Sinuate: to curve back and forth, to wind

V **Naivest:** superlative of **naive:** credulous, lacking worldy experience

Natives: plural of **native:** an inhabitant by birth of a place

Vainest: superlative of **vain:** overly prideful of onself

W **Tawnies:** plural of **tawny:** a yellowish-brown color

Waniest: superlative of **wany:** visibly decreasing in size (also **waney**)

X **Antisex:** antagonistic toward sexual activity

Sextain: a six-line stanza

Z **Zeatins:** plural of **zeatin:** a plant hormone found in corn and coconut milk

Zaniest: superlative of **zany:** wacky

The other incredible six-tile combo to be on the lookout for is AEINRT, more easily remembered as RETAIN. They're common letters that, when combined with a blank or one of the following letters, are capable of producing more than fifty bingos (including the nine in the previous list that make up **tisane**+r). It's worthwhile being able to recognize them.

RETAIN plus:

C **Ceratin:** a fibrous protein found in hair, nails, claws, hooves, and horns (also **keratin**)

Certain: confident

Creatin: an organic compound that supplies energy to cells (also **creatine**)

D **Antired:** anticommunist

Detrain: to disembark from a railroad train

Trained: past tense of **train:** to instruct manually

E **Arenite:** a sedimentary rock

Retinae: plural of **retina:** a light-sensitive membrane of the eye (also **retinas**)

Trainee: one who is being trained

F **Fainter:** one who faints, or a comparative of **faint:** weak, languid

G **Granite:** a common igneous rock

Gratine: encrusted (**gratin** *is a type of food crust,* **gratine** *is the adjective,* **gratinee** *is the verb*)

Ingrate: one who is not appreciative or thankful

Tangier: comparative of **tangy:** having a strong sour or citrus taste or aftertaste

Tearing: present tense of **tear:** to emit tears from the eye; or present tense of **tear:** to rip

H **Hairnet:** a net worn on the head to confine hair

Inearth: to bury or inter

I **Inertia:** resistance to a change in motion or stillness

K **Keratin:** a fibrous protein found in hair, nails, claws, hooves, and horns (also **ceratin**)

L **Latrine:** a communal toilet

Ratline: a horizaontal rope used as part of **ratlines**, a set of ropes tied together on a ship to create a large rope ladder used to adjust sails and as a lookout (*pronounced "rattlin"*)

Reliant: exhibiting reliance

Retinal: a pigment found in the retina (also **retinene**)

Trenail: a wooden peg used to fasten timber in shipbuilding (also **treenail**) (*As treenails are made of wood, they expand when exposed to moisture, creating a secure hold.*)

M **Minaret:** a tall, conical spire that is typically attached to a mosque
Raiment: clothes
N **Entrain:** to board a train
P **Painter:** one who paints
Pertain: to refer or relate to
Repaint: to paint again
R **Retrain:** to train again
Terrain: geographical landscape
Trainer: one who trains
S **Anestri:** plural of **anestrus:** a period of sexual dormancy in cyclically breeding mammals
Antsier: comparative of **antsy:** nervous, restless
Nastier: comparative of **nasty:** mean, wicked
Ratines: plural of **ratine:** a rough fabric that is loosely woven
Retains: present tense of **retain:** to continue to possess
Retinas: plural of **retina:** a light-sensitive membrane of the eye (also **retinae**)
Retsina: a Greek wine
Stainer: one who stains
Stearin: a triglyceride used to make candles and soap
T **Intreat:** to beseech (also **entreat**)
Iterant: repeating
Nattier: comparative of **natty:** sharply attired
Nitrate: to apply nitric acid
Tertian: a severe, recurrent two-day fever typical of malaria
U **Taurine:** an organic acid found in animal tissues
Uranite: a radioactive, uranium-rich mineral (also *uraninite*)
Urinate: to discharge urine
W **Tawnier:** comparative of **tawny:** yellow-brown in color
Tinware: an article, such as housewares, made of tinplate

PART 3

The Lexicon Contextualized:
Speaking Scrabblish

Now it's time to have a little fun. It's one thing to look over lists of related playable words, but words without sentences are notes without a song. To indulge the ulna (bone often thought of as the funny bone), the following example sentences and tongue twisters string together some of the best bits of the Scrabble lexicon. It's worth noting that just as Scrabblish is made of a lot of somewhat silly words, the following sentences are presented primarily for fun. While efforts have been made to use each word in an as-near-to-accurate way as possible, these examples are not intended to display model usage, but rather to suggest a sense of the words' meanings.

The **aa** formed the **maar** that you can see through the **haar**.
But the natives, who **craal** their **baaing** sheep and fish from a
praam out at the **haaf**, credit a **baal**.

Aa: a type of stony, rough lava
Maar: a volcanic crater
Haar: a fog
Craal: to pen in an animal (also **kraal**)
Baa: to make a bleating sound
Praam: a flat-bottomed boat (also **pram**)
Haaf: a deep-sea fishing ground found far offshore
Baal: any of several Canaanite or Phoenician gods

Abed in the **abri**, **abba**'s **aba**, like an **alb**, hid his **abs**.

Abed: laying in bed
Abri: a bomb shelter
Abba: a father
Aba: a traditional sleeveless garment worn by Arab men
Alb: a full-length white vestment
Ab: an abdominal muscle

Ae blae kae with **twae alae hae nae wae** if it **lek**s well.

Ae: one (adj.)
Blae: bluish-black in color
Kae: a bird similar to the crow, also known as the jackdaw or
grackle
Twae: two
Alae: plural of **ala:** a wing or similar appendage
Hae: to have (**haed, haen, haeing, haes**)
Nae: no or not
Wae: woe
Lek: a currency of Albania (pl. **leks** or **leke** or **leku**) or (v.)
to present a competitive mating display (*as, for example, the
grackle does*)

Nan saw **lac** on the insect's **ala** she found in the **nala.** She looked it up in the **ana** as she ate **nan.**

Lac: a red resin secreted by some insects
Ala: a wing (pl. **alae**)
Nala: a steep narrow valley or ravine (also **nullah**)
Ana: a collection of miscellany about a specific topic
Nan: a leavened flatbread (also **naan**)

The **aga** was stricken with **ague**, so he threw his **aggie agly.**

Aga: a Turkish military commander (also **agha**)
Ague: a fever associated with malaria
Aggie: a type of marble
Agly: awry (also **agley, aglee**)

Ali, who was **anile**, strolled down the **allee** past an **aalii, anil, aal**, and **al.**

Anile: resembling an old and/or senile woman
Allee: a tree-lined path
Aalii: a type of tropical tree
Anil: a type of West Indian plant
Aal: a type of East Indian shrub
Al: a type of East Indian tree

If I told you once, I told you **bis**—don't build a **burg** on a **berg.**

Bis: twice, again, *or* plural of **bi** (*as in the wonderful Latin phrase* "bis dat qui cito dat": "*he gives twice who gives promptly*")
Burg: a town or city
Berg: an iceberg

B

The **bawd** in **braw braws busk**s to **buss** her **beau.**

Bawd: a female head of a brothel
Braw: excellent
Braws: (n./pl.) fine clothing

Busk: to prepare
Buss: to kiss
Beau: a boyfriend (pl. **beaux**)

The **babu** beneath the **babul** eats **baba**, but the **baboo** in the **babool** prefers **babka**. Amidst the **babel**, the **bub** with a **bubo** rides a **bubal** by the **babassu**.

Babu: Hindu gentleman (also **baboo**)
Babul: the acacia tree (also **babool**)
Baba: a cake steeped in rum
Baboo: babu
Babool: babul
Babka: a type of coffee cake
Babel: confused ruckus
Bub: a young man, particularly an upstart
Bubo: a swollen lymph node in the groin or armpit
Bubal: a type of large antelope now extinct
Babassu: a palm tree that yields an edible oil

The **baldy** bet the **berk** a bag of **bani** that the **bairn** couldn't **banjax** the **bankit** with a **baffy**.

Baldy: one who is bald
Berk: a fool
Bani: a Romanian monetary unit (pl. **ban**)
Bairn: a child
Banjax: to damage or destroy
Bankit: a raised sidewalk, used in the American South (also **banquette**)
Baffy: the 4 wood golf club

In the **bazar**, near the baskets of **braize**, the **bozo** pays big **baizas** for **brazas** of **baize**.

Bazar: a marketplace (also **bazaar**)
Braize: a European marine fish
Bozo: a fool

Baiza: an Omani monetary unit
Braza: a Spanish unit of length, equal to almost 1⅔ meters
Baize: the coarse, woolen fabric used on billiards tables, similar to felt

If sheep on the **brae brux** when they **blat**, they may have **braxy**.

Brae: a slope or hillside
Brux: to grind the teeth (the noun is **bruxism**)
Baa: to bleat
Blat: to bleat
Braxy: a disease of sheep

In the **botel**, the **bucko bungs** the **bot** in the **bota** with **batt** he'd bought for four **baht**.

Botel: a floating hotel (also **boatel**, **floatel**)
Bucko: a bully or ruffian
Bung: to plug with a cork or stopper
Bot: the larva of a botfly (also **bott**)
Bota: a leather bottle, usually used for wine
Batt: cotton used for stuffing quilts and sleeping bags
Baht: a monetary unit of Thailand, worth about three American cents

---

Care to **coff** some **cole** or **cos**, **coz**? I accept **chon, chao, cory**, and **cedi**.

Coff: to buy (chiefly Scottish)
Cole: kale (also **kail**)
Cos: romaine lettuce
Coz: a cousin (pl. **cozes** or **cozzes**)
Chon: the monetary unit of South Korea
Chao: "a monetary unit of Vietnam" according to the *OSPD*
Cory: "a former monetary unit of Guinea" according to the *OSPD*
Cedi: the basic monetary unit of Ghana

"Ciao," said the **chic chica** by the **chico** to the **chicer chola**
by the **casa**.

Ciao: an expression of greeting or departure
Chic: stylish or (n.) stylishness
Chica: a girl or young woman
Chico: a common shrub in the American west, known as the
greasewood
Chicer: more stylish
Chola: a Mexican American girl
Casa: a house

He heard the **coon, cony, cavy,** and **chipmuck chirk, chirm,**
and **chirr.**

Coon: a raccoon
Cony: a rabbit
Cavy: a short-tailed rodent found in South America
Chipmuck: a chipmunk
Chirk: to make a shrill noise like a small animal, or (adj.) happy
Chirm: to chirp like a bird
Chirr: to chirp like an insect (also **chirre**)

The *OSPD* includes **cholo** (defined as a "pachuco") and **chola** ("a
Mexican American girl"). **Pachuco,** "a flashy Mexican American
youth," is also playable. The term *cholo* dates back to at least the
early seventeenth century, when it was defined in a Peruvian book
as a word for a child of mixed black and indigenous Indian heritage:
"it means *dog*, not of the purebred variety, but of very disreputable
origin; and the Spaniards use it for insult and vituperation."

In recent years, *cholo* and *chola* have been somewhat *reappro-
priated*, and are used self-descriptively by southwestern
Americans of Mexican descent who identify with the general
styles and/or ethos of youth culture found in hip-hop and/or
gangsta scenes.

The **cadi** and **caid** count the **cain**.

Cadi: a judge in Islamic courts (also **kadi, qadi**)
Caid: a Muslim chieftain (also **qaid**)
Cain: rent for land paid in produce or livestock (also **kain**)

The **coot** and the **cooter** are **snooty** to the **cootie** and **crappy** to the **crappie**.

Coot: a dark-gray aquatic bird
Cooter: any of many freshwater turtles common in the eastern United States (*from* kuta, *the Malian word for turtle*)
Snooty: snobbish
Cootie: a body louse
Crappy: decidedly bad
Crappie: a common freshwater food fish

Don't **cark** about the **carb**—just don't **clag** the **cam**.

Cark: to worry
Carb: a carburetor
Clag: to clog
Cam: a rotating or sliding piece of machinery

The **cobby kob stob**s the **cobb** near the **dobby**'s **doby**.

Cobby: stocky (used of animals)
Kob: an orange-brown antelope
Stob: to stab
Cobb: a sea gull
Dobby: a foolish old man
Doby: adobe (also **dobie**)

The **dorty dork** in the **doty dory** takes his **dore dor** to the **dorp**.

Dorty: sulky
Dork: a socially inept person, an outsider (*It's likely that* dork, *which can also mean "penis," became* dick.)

Doty: marked by decay
Dory: a small, flat-bottomed boat found in New England
Dore: gilded
Dor: a European beetle (also **dorr, dorbug**)
Dorp: a village (chiefly South African)

The **drys durn** the drunks who **dram**.
They even **drat** and **dang** the **dreg** to the **deil**.

Dry: a prohibitionist (-s)
Durn: to damn
Dram: to drink alcohol
Drat: to damn
Dang: to damn
Dreg: the sediment of alcoholic beverages
Deil: the devil

"It's **dere, doc**," says the **dona**, a former **def deb** from a **deme** in the **dene**. "I can't **dure** the **dol**s in my **derm**."

Dere: dire
Doc: doctor
Dona: a respected Spanish lady
Def: excellent (**deffer, deffest**)
Deb: a debutante
Deme: a district in Greece
Dene: a valley
Dure: to endure
Dol: a unit of pain intensity equal to one "just noticeable difference" (JND) of pain (*Developed at Cornell University in the mid-twentieth century, the dol is no longer used.*)
Derm: the skin (also **derma**)

My **eme** Ed may only have an **elhi ed**—he's no **einstein**—but he knows an **edh** from an **eng**.

Eme: uncle or an avuncular person (Scottish)
Elhi: relating to school grades 1 through 12
Ed: education
Einstein: a very intelligent person
Edh: a letter in Old English, Icelandic, and Faeroese (also **eth**)
Eng: a Latin letter

The **ecru euro** has had **enow eau**.

Ecru: a color similar to beige
Euro: an Australian marsupial
Enow: enough
Eau: water (pl. **eaux**)

"The **eyas's eyry** was **erst** the **eyass's**," the **ern** told the **eyra**.

Eyas: a young hawk
Eyry: the lofty nest of a bird of prey (also **aerie**, **eyrie**)
Erst: formerly, long ago
Eyass: a falcon (*defined in the* OSPD *as an* **eyas**, *but they're gener-
ally considered to have slightly different meanings*)
Ern: a sea eagle (also **erne**)
Eyra: an American wildcat

Because of his **eld**, it's less **eath** for the **ebbet** to climb the **ers**.

Eld: old age
Eath: easy (Scottish)
Ebbet: a green newt also known as a spring peeper
Ers: a climbing plant (also **ervil**)

Fie, you won't **fob** me with that **faux fido**—it's just a **fil**! **Foh**, it's a **fico**—you can't **fub** me. I'm no **feeb**!

Fie: an exclamation of disapproval
Fob: to deceive or cheat (also **fub**)
Faux: fake
Fido: an irregular coin
Fil: a coin of little value found in many Middle East countries
Foh: an exclamation of disgust (also **faugh**)
Fico: a trifle, something almost worthless
Fub: to deceive or cheat (also **fob**)
Feeb: a feebleminded person

The **deft ganef** in the **weft reft** the **kef** from the **eft** and **eftsoon** left as he **cleft** the **teff**.

Deft: skillful in movements
Ganef: a thief (also **gonef, ganof, gonof, gonoph, gonif**, and **goniff**)
Weft: a type of specially woven fabric or garment
Reft: past tense of **reave**: to seize, to forcibly plunder
Kef: hemp smoked to euphoria (also **kif, kaif, keef, kief**)
Eft: a newt
Eftsoon: soon after (also **eftsoons**)
Cleft: past tense of **cleave**: to split
Teff: an African cereal grass

The **fice** was **fain** to **fet** the **fez fer** the **fud**.

Fice: a small dog of mixed breed (also **fyce, feist**)
Fain: pleased, particularly to do something
Fet: to fetch
Fez: a brimless hat worn by men in Turkey
Fer: for
Fud: old-fashioned, stuffy person

Since it **fash**es the **fiar**, a **fiat** forbids **fifing** in the **fief**.

Fash: to bother
Fiar: a landowner in Scottish law
Fiat: an order or decree
Fife: to play a sort of high-pitched flute
Fief: a feudal estate

Fess to the **fed**s or I'll **fink**!

Fess: to confess
Fed: a federal agent
Fink: to inform the authorities on someone

The **giglet** did a **giga** with the **piglet**, **eaglet**, **auklet**, **swiftlet**, and **owlet**.

Giglet: a playful young girl (also **giglot**)
Giga: a lively dance that evolved from the jig (pl. **gighe**)
(also **gigue**)
Piglet: a young pig
Eaglet: a young eagle

G

Auklet: a young auk
Swiftlet: a Pacific swift, known for using saliva to help build its nest (*Their nests are a Chinese delicacy used in soups and are among the most expensive edible products eaten by humans. A bowl of bird's nest soup can cost $100, and a kilogram of bird's nest can run up to $10,000.*)
Owlet: a young or small owl

Wine **guggle**d from **guglet**s and **goglet**s as Gil grilled a **gigot**.

Guggle: to flow unevenly, producing a soft noise (also **gurgle**)
Guglet: a long-necked vessel of earthenware (also **goglet**)
Gigot: a mutton leg

The **saiga**'s **amiga** hates the **taiga**.

Saiga: a critically endangered tundra antelope
Amiga: a female friend
Taiga: a subarctic forest of firs and spruces

The **gleg grig glug**s **grog** in the **grot**.

Gleg: alert and quick to respond (Scottish)
Grig: a lively, animated person
Glug: to make a gurgling sound by drinking or pouring
Grog: a mixture of liquor and water; beer
Grot: a grotto

Yerk the **yegg**; if you **igg** him he'll **nim** the **migg**.

Yerk: to beat vigorously through strikes, stabs, kicks, etc.
Yegg: a thief, particularly a burglar
Igg: to ignore
Nim: to steal
Migg: a type of playing marble (also **mig**, **miggle**)

If he drinks a **noggin** of **nogg**, the **hogg** will **mugg** and play with the **piggin** behind the **biggin**.

Noggin: a small amount of liquor
Nogg: a type of strong ale
Hogg: a young sheep before it's shorn
Mugg: to make a funny face
Piggin: a small wooden bucket
Biggin: a house or cottage

The **glumpy gled glime**s the **glim**—he'll **glom** it in a **gliff**.

Glumpy: glum or sulky
Gled: a bird of prey also known as the kite (also **glede**)
Glime: to glance at slyly
Glim: a light or lamp, or an eye (*To "douse the glim" means both "to put out the light" and "to punch someone in the eye"—just as in "knock someone's lights out."*)
Glom: to steal
Gliff: a brief moment; or a sudden sight of something that startles

"**Voila**," said the pitcher.
"**Um . . . ,**" said the **ump**, "**umm . . . uh . . . eh . . . hm . . . hmm . . .**"
"**Hunh**?" said the catcher.
"**Ahem**," said the batter.
"**Eureka**," said the umpire. "Strike three!"
"**Huh**?" Said the batter.
"**Mm**," said the pitcher.
"**Ah!**" "**Aah!**" "**Aha!**" "**Hah!**" "**Ha!**" "**Ooh!**" "**Ho!**" "**Oho!**"
Everyone **oh**ed. Except the **boobirds**—who **boo**ed.

Voila: used to call attention to something
Um: an expression of hesitation (also **umm**)
Ump: to umpire a baseball game; an umpire
Umm: an expression of hesitation (also **um**)
Uh: used to express hesitation
Eh: used to express doubt
Hm: an expression of thoughtful consideration (also **hmm**)
Hmm: used to express thoughtful consideration (also **hm**)
Hunh: an expression requesting the repetition of something said
Ahem: used to attract attention
Eureka: used to express triumph upon discovering something

Huh: used to express surprise
Mm: used to express appreciation or assent
Ah: aah
Aah: to exclaim in amazement, joy, or surprise
Aha: an expression of surprise, accomplishment, or mockery
Hah: ha
Ha: a sound of surprise
Ooh: to exclaim in amazement, joy, or surprise
Ho: used to express surprise
Oho: an interjection expressing surprise
Oh: to exclaim surprise, pain, or desire
Boobird: a fan who boos players on the home team
Boo: to cry "boo"

Let's **hongi** by the **honan hong, hon.**

Hongi: to greet another by pressing together noses (**hongiing**)
Honan: a fine silk
Hong: a Chinese factory
Hon: a sweetheart (also **honeybun**)

Eyeing the **ilea, ilia,** and **inia** made Ira **inly** feel **illy** and **iffy.**

Ilea: plural of **ileum:** a part of the small intestine
Ilia: plural of **ilium:** a bone in the pelvis
Inia: a part of the skull
Inly: inwardly
Illy: badly
Iffy: full of ifs, uncertain

Iris put **ilex** and **ixia** inside **ilka isba.**

Ilex: a genus of plant that includes holly
Ixia: a South African iris
Ilka: every
Isba: a Russian log cabin

The **genii** in the **torii** extend their **medii** at the **impli.**

Genii: plural of **genius:** a person of exceptional intelligence
Torii: a gateway to a Shinto temple
Medii: plural of **medius:** the middle finger
Impli: a band of Zulu warriors

Iwis, the **jus** of the **ibis** in the **mid** of the **miri** is **nisi.**

Iwis: certainly (also **ywis**)
Jus: a legal right
Ibis: a long-legged wading bird
Mid: middle
Miri: plural of **mir:** a Russian peasant compound
Nisi: not yet final, to be enacted depending upon unresolved factors

The **biddy** in a **midi** smokes a **bidi** beside the **tipi.**

Biddy: literally a hen, also used figuratively for an old woman
Midi: a type of skirt or coat that extends to the middle of the calf
Bidi: a cigarette of India (also **beedi**)
Tipi: tepee (also **teepee**)

At the **ceili,** Billy told me it'll be ten **intis** or seven **sylis** to fix the **tali** of my **puli.**

Ceili: a Gaelic social gathering or party (also **ceilidh**)
Inti: a former currency of Peru
Syli: a former monetary unit of Guinea
Tali: plural of **talus:** a bone in the ankle
Puli: a long-haired sheepdog known for its corded coat (pl. **pulis** or **pulik**)

The **joe**'s **jo**'s **jenny jib**s at the sight of the **jocko** and tries to **jink**.

Joe: a guy
Jo: a sweetheart
Jenny: a female donkey
Jib: to refuse to proceed further or comply
Jocko: a chimpanzee or monkey
Jink: to move out of the way, to change direction

An Irregular Joe

Like **qi** and **za**, **jo** is an invaluable word to have in your arsenal. **Jo**—a sweetheart—is by far the easiest way to unload the J for quick points. But beware: there is no jos. The plural, like the plural of **joe** (a guy) is **joes**.

The **juco coed** at the **juku** dance did the **kolo**, the **juba**, and the **jota**.

Juco: junior college
Coed: a female college student
Juku: a school in Japan that readies students for college
Kolo: a Serbian folk dance
Juba: a lively dance born on Southern slave plantations
Jota: a folk dance from northern Spain

The **jerry** in the **johnny jape**d the **jane**'s **jupe** and **jibe**d the **jabot** on her **joseph**.

Jerry: a German soldier
Johnny: a hospital gown
Jape: to play a joke upon or mock
Jane: a woman or girl
Jupe: a woman's short jacket

Jibe: to jeer (also **gibe**)
Jabot: a decoration on a shirt, like a frill or ruffle
Joseph: a woman's long cloak

The **jehu**, a **jefe**, didn't **jauk**; he was there in a **jiff**.

Jehu: a fast, furious driver
Jefe: a chief
Jauk: to dally
Jiff: jiffy, instant

The **haji** in a **taj jee**s on his **haj** to the religious **mecca**.

Haji: one making a haj (also **hadji** and **hadjee**)
Taj: a tall, conical hat worn in some Islamic countries
Jee: to go to the right (also **gee**) (also **ajee**, meaning "off to the side")
Haj: a pilgrimage to **Mecca** (also **hadj**, **hajj**)
Mecca: an important destination for many people

Scott, a **scop**, and Sigrun, a **skald**, **kip** atop the **kop**.

Scop: an Old English poet
Skald: an Old Norse poet
Kip: to sleep
Kop: an isolated hill (also **kopje**)

Ken **ken**s **kendo** but prefers **keno**.

Ken: to know
Kendo: a modern Japanese martial art involving swords (**Kendo** *literally means "Way of the Sword."*)
Keno: a game of chance like lotto popular in casinos (**Keno** *offers perhaps the worst odds of return of any game offered at most casinos.*)

The Ki to the Kay: K Words

Thanks be to world religions, who give us two easy ways to drop the K: **ki**, the life force in Chinese culture, pronounced "chee" (also **qi**), and **ka** the eternal soul in ancient Egyptian religion.

The **cate**, a cake, is so small it won't **sate** or even **bate** Kate's appetite. It's like eating **tate**. She should have made a **bisk** of **torsk** or **cusk**, or a **rusk**. And if she kept up her **kata**, it wouldn't go to her **nates**.

Cate: a choice food or delicacy
Sate: to satiate
Bate: to lessen
Tate: a tuft of hair
Bisk: bisque
Torsk: a large marine food fish also known as cusk, opah, or moonfish
Cusk: a large marine food fish also known as torsk, opah, or moonfish
Rusk: a light biscuit, often as baby food
Kata: a set of movements in several different Japanese martial arts
Nates: (n./pl.) the buttocks

For ten **taka** and one **marka**, the **makar** bought the **abaka** from the **kabaka**.

Taka: the currency of Bangladesh
Marka: the currency of Bosnia and Herzegovina
Makar: a poet (Scottish)
Abaka: a Philippine cultivar of banana (also **abaca**)
Kabaka: the king of Buganda, a subnational kingdom of Uganda

The **luckie** was a **sickie**, but her **dickie** was **duckie**.

Luckie: an affectionate term for an old woman (*Archaic terms for one's grandparents include* lucky-minnie *for grandmother and* lucky-daddie *for grandfather.*)
Sickie: a person of perverted tastes (also **sicko** and **phyco**)
Dickie: a detachable shirt or blouse front (also **dicky**, **dickey**)
Duckie: excellent (also **ducky**)

In the **mirk** near the **kirk**, Kirk **dirk**s Dirk Burke, then **burke**s him by the **birk**.

Mirk: dark, or darkness (also **murk**)
Kirk: a church
Dirk: to stab with a small knife (Dirk *has also been traced back to the word* dick *to mean "a penis."*)
Burke: to murder by strangulation, or to smother/hush someone (*Coined after the serial killer William Burke who, with his partner, suffocated seventeen victims in order to sell the corpses for medical dissection. Burke himself was hanged.*)
Birk: a birch tree

The **stirk** in the **sark** and the **koel** in **kohl** drink **kir** and **kola** with the **mola**.

Stirk: a yearling bull or cow

Sark: a shirt
Koel: a cuckoo of the Eastern hemisphere
Kohl: a type of black powder used as eye makeup
Kir: an aperitif of white wine and black currant liqueur popular in France (*named after Félix Kir, a former mayor of Dijon*)
Kola: cola
Mola: an enormous marine fish that typically weighs more than a ton, also known as the ocean sunfish

---

Lo! Lee **lam**s up the **lum** and legs it **levo** a **li** to the **lea**.

Lo: (interjection) used to attract attention
Lam: to flee
Lum: chimney
Levo: toward the left
Li: a Chinese unit of distance equal to .4 miles
Lea: a meadow (also **ley**)

With **elan**, the **alan gae**s **alane alang** the **lang** lane.

Elan: style and enthusiasm
Alan: a breed of hunting dog, named after the Alan people (also **aland, alant**)
Gae: to go (**gaed, gane** or **gaen, gaeing, gaun, gaes**)
Alane: alone
Alang: along
Lang: long

Louie, a **luny louie** without a **leu** or **lev**, **levant**s to the Levant.

Luny: loony (adj. and n.)
Louie: a lieutenant (also **looie**)
Leu: the currency of Moldova and Romania (pl. **lei**)
Lev: the currency of Bulgaria
Levant: to abscond in order to avoid a debt

> The **motmot** in the **mott** made a **mot** about the **motet**.

Motmot: a colorful, long-tailed bird native to Central and South America
Mott: a small cluster of trees, typically on a prairie (also **motte**)
Mot: a witty remark
Motet: a type of choral composition involving a sacred text

> The **mod** in the **mag** for **modish ma**s wears a **mac**, one **moc**, and one **pac**.

Mod: a stylish person
Mag: a magazine
Modish: stylish
Ma: mother
Mac: a raincoat (also **mack**, **mackintosh**)
Moc: a moccasin
Pac: an insulated, waterproof, laced boot originally made by Native Americans (also **shoepack**)

> The **mim moll** models a **mongo mobcap** for her **mon**.

Mim: prim, overly meek
Moll: a gangster's girlfriend

Mongo: low-grade wool, often used as rags (also **mongoe**,
mungo)
Mobcap: a large cap worn indoors by married women in the
eighteenth century
Mon: man

It's the **mozo**'s **moira** to **moil** for **mony momes**.

Mozo: a manual laborer (*in the southwestern United States*)
Moira: fate or destiny, in Greek mythology
Moil: to work hard
Mony: many (also **monie**)
Mome: a fool, a dull or silent person with nothing to say

The **mopy moppet** made a **moue** at the **roue** with her
mammy.

Mopy: mopey
Moppet: a child
Moue: a pouting expression
Roue: a lecherous old man
Mammy: mother

Watch the **mamba mambo** and **samba**, **embow**ing his back
(he's got no **gamb**s) to the **gamba** and **mbira**.

Mamba: a venomous African snake
Mambo: to perform a Latin American dance like the rumba
Samba: to perform a Brazilian dance of African origin
Embow: to arch or vault
Gamb: the leg of animal, particularly when depicted on a coat
of arms
Gamba: a bass viol, sounding approximately like a cello
Mbira: an African musical instrument made of a base with strips
that resonate when plucked, also known as the thumb piano

At **neap**, my **netop**—a **neatnik** who's a **naif**—tried to **nett nekton** from the **ness** by the **linn** for the **nth** time. Again: **nada.**

Neap: a tide halfway between high and low tides
Netop: a buddy
Neatnik: a compulsively neat person
Naif: a naive person
Nett: to net
Nekton: any free-swimming aquatic animals (*in contrast with* **plankton**)
Ness: a headland
Linn: a waterfall (also **lin**)
Nth: describing an unspecified number of a series
Nada: nothing

Neist, he ate a **neep** on a **bunn** and a **nutlet** and nabbed a **neg** of a **neb** of a **nene** from a **neuk**.

Neist: next
Neep: a turnip
Bunn: bun
Nutlet: a small nut
Neg: a photographic negative
Neb: a bird's beak
Nene: a rare, wild Hawaiian goose
Neuk: a nook

A **yob** by the **nom** of Bob, **ne** Robert, **hob**s the shoe of a **nob**—a **nawab** named Bobo, **nee** Roberta.

Yob: a hoodlum (Yob *is an example of* <u>backslang</u>—*a backward construction of* boy.)
Nom: a name
Ne: born with the name of, for a male
Hob: to put hobnails on a shoe
Nob: a rich person

Nawab: a rich and prominent person, or one who acts in that fashion (also **nabob**, **nabobess** [f])

Nee: born with the name of, for a female

"You call this **broo**, **bro**?" the **boor pooh**ed. "I call it **goo**, **goop**, **gook**, **gunk**. But it sure ain't **bree**."

Broo: a broth (also **bree**)
Bro: brother
Boor: an ill-mannered person
Pooh: to express contempt for
Goo: a sticky or slimy substance, often a residue of unknown origin (also **gook**)
Goop: a heavy, unpleasant liquid
Gook: a sticky or slimy substance, often a residue of unknown origin (also **goo**)
Gunk: a sticky, greasy, or unpleasant substance, often clogging a small space
Bree: broth (also **broo**)

For a **kobo**, the **lobo** buys a **gobo** for his **bo**, a **goby** in his **toby**.

Kobo: a small unit of Nigerian currency
Lobo: a timber wolf
Gobo: a shield to block extraneous noise from a microphone
Bo: a buddy
Goby: a very small fish that has fused pelvic fins that create a suction cup
Toby: a drinking mug in the shape of a man or a man's face

It's **soth**: the **wroth goth doth loth** his **mothy bothy**.

Soth: true (also **sooth**)
Wroth: very angry
Goth: a morose style of music, or a maker or fan of such music
Doth: an antiquated third-person present form of do

A Tip from Prof. Wagstaff of Huxley College

One used to be said to "wax **wroth**," or grow angry, which is fodder for one of the great Groucho Marx lines in *Horse Feathers*:

Secretary: "The Dean is furious. He's waxing wroth."

Groucho: "Is Roth out there too? Tell Roth to wax the Dean for a while."

Loth: loath
Mothy: abounding in moths
Bothy: a basic shelter left open for common use, particularly in Scotland

The **kea** in the **koa**, like the **boa, goa, moa,** and **anoa,** are all **zoa.**

Kea: a species of New Zealand parrot known for its exceptional intelligence
Koa: a flowering Hawaiian tree
Boa: a large nonvenomous snake that constricts its prey
Goa: a Tibetan gazelle
Moa: an extinct flightless bird of New Zealand
Anoa: the dwarf buffalo of Indonesia
Zoa: plural of **zoon:** the whole product of a single fertilized egg

"I'll have the **coho** with some **pepo** and **sybo,**" ordered the **boho.** "Oh, and some **vino.**"

Coho: the North Pacific silver salmon
Pepo: any fruit having a fleshy interior and a hard rind, including melons and cucumbers
Sybo: a variety of onion also known as the Welsh onion (also **cibol**)
Boho: a bohemian
Vino: wine

Look at this **yahoo** trying to **shoo** the **hoopoe**. **"Skidoo, git oot noo!"** he **cooee**s.

Yahoo: a coarse, easily excited person
Shoo: to drive off
Hoopoe: a colorful bird with distinctive plumage on its head
Skidoo: to leave quickly (also **skiddo**)
Git: to get
Oot: out
Noo: now
Cooee: to cry out loudly in order to gain attention, particularly in the Australian outback (also **cooey**)

"Pfui!"
"Pah! Poh!"

Pfui: phooey
Pah: an exclamation of disgust
Poh: an expression of disapproval (also **pugh**)

On the shelf next to the **pye** and the **pyx** is a **pic** of the priest receiving the **pax** from the holy **pa**.

Pye: a former book of ecclesiastical rules in the Church of England

Pyx: a container for the Eucharist (also **pix**)
Pic: a photograph
Pax: a ceremonial kissing of a tablet at a Christian mass; the kiss of peace
Pa: a father

People with **pica** probably won't eat **paca**, or **spica**, or even an **orca**'s **plica**—they might prefer **mica**.

Pica: a medical disorder involving the craving to eat things that are not food
Paca: a large rodent considered a delicacy in Central and South America
Spica: an ear of corn (pl. **spica** or **spicae**)
Orca: the killer whale (also **orc**)
Plica: a fold of skin
Mica: a type of mineral that is easily cleaved along structural planes

Yep, the **klepht** wearing the **kepi** sure can **kep** a bee from a **skep** or a **kelep** from under a **cep**.

Yep: yes
Klepht: a Greek guerrilla who lived in the mountains of the Ottoman Empire and resisted Ottoman rule between the fifteenth and nineteenth centuries
Kepi: a type of cap primarily used by the French and American militaries during the nineteenth and early twentieth centuries
Kep: to catch (archaic Scots)
Skep: a handwoven beehive, often of wicker
Kelep: a stinging ant found in Central America
Cep: a type of large mushroom (also **cepe**)

The **grampus** holds a **gamp** for the **gramp grumphy**, who **gimp**s and **grump**s.

Grampus: the orca
Gamp: a large, bulky umbrella (chiefly British)

Gramp: a grandfather
Grumphy: a familiar name for a pig (also **grumphie**) (chiefly Scottish)
Gimp: to limp
Grump: to complain or sulk

The **tampan tamp**s the **samp** on the **sampan.**

Tampan: a biting African tick
Tamp: to pack down or compress with repeated taps
Samp: coarsely ground maize, often used for porridge
Sampan: a flat-bottomed Chinese boat

The **quean** in the **quod** says she'd love a quart of **quass**.
"**Quotha**! and I'll have an **usque** and **aquae**," **squib**s the **squab**.

Quean: a prostitute
Quod: a jail
Quass: a Russian beer made of fermented rye bread (also **kvas, kvass**)
Quotha: an expression of sarcasm or surprise
Usque: whiskey (also **usquebae**) (*from the Gaelic* usquebaugh, *meaning "water of life"*)
Aquae: plural of **aqua:** water
Squib: to satirize
Squab: a juvenile pigeon

The **equid, quey, quokka,** and **quagga** are in a **qaug** near the **quai.**

Equid: any animal of the Equidae family, including horses, donkeys, and zebras
Quey: a heifer
Quokka: a short-tailed, cat-sized wallaby
Quagga: an extinct zebralike animal with the front of the body resembling a zebra and the back resembling a horse (*Efforts are under way to selectively "back-breed" the quagga into existence. This is different from the* **zebroid/zebrass** *or the* **zebrine,** *the specific offspring of a female zebra and a male horse.*)
Quag: a bog
Quai: a wharf or pier (also **quay**)

The **quale** of having a **quint** of **quate quin**s **quant** is **quare.**

Quale: the singular way it feels to experience a particular mental state
Quint: a sequence or set of five
Quate: quiet
Quin: a quintuplet

Quant: to propel a barge or boat through water with a pole
Quare: queer

"As a **tuque** is not even a **quasi toque**, the **quoit** is not **roque**."
quoth the **quango.**

Tuque: a tight-fitting knit cap, as worn by sailors
Quasi: somewhat like
Toque: a close-fitting, tall, cylindrical hat popular with cooks
Quoit: to toss a ring in quoits, a throwing game like horseshoes
and ring toss (*usually played outdoors, but one can find* **quoit** *played
indoors in an altered, table version in Wales and western England*)
Roque: an American form of croquet (**Roque** *was actually an
Olympic sport for just one Olympics, in 1904 in St. Louis, at which time
it was being hailed as "the game of the century."*)
Quoth: said (**Quoth** *is an unusual verb as it's to be used only before
the subject.*)
Quango: a quasi-autonomous nongovernmental organization,
found in the United Kingdom

The **quipu**, **qua** calculator, could count **qursh.**

Quipu: an intricate Inca calculating device making use of knotted
llama or alpaca hair (also **quippu**)
Qua: in the capacity of
Qursh: a currency of Saudi Arabia equal to one-twentieth of a
riyal (also **qurush**, **girsh**, **gursh**)

My **nuncle**, a **quidnunc**, **quirts** a **quezal** in a **squill.**

Nuncle: an uncle (*from an archaic combination of mine and uncle,
as in* King Lear: *"I have us'd it, nuncle, ever since thou mad'st thy
daughters thy mother."*)
Quidnunc: a gossip
Quirt: to strike with a rawhide whip that forks into two tails at
the end
Quezal: a bright green tropical bird (also **quetzal**)
Squill: a flowering bulb native to the Mediterranean

"With or Without U"

In UpWords, the Q tile is a little friendlier, as it actually contains a *u* on it. But in Scrabble, Anagrams, and the like, it helps to know the approximately fifteen words in the *OSPD* that use a Q but don't require a U.

Here's a song to help you remember them. (Sung to the tune of U2's "With or Without You." Sadly, <u>bono</u> is not a word, but **bonobo** is. Also, look what four letters are hidden in **nutwood**.)

> See the tiles there on the board
> See all the ways I might have scored
> I'll wait for U.
>
> Sleight of hand and twist of fate
> On a rack of wood Q makes me wait
> And I wait without U.
>
> With or without U.
> With or without U.
>
> From the bag, I'd drawn out four
> It gave me Q but I want more
> And I'm waiting for U.
>
> With or without U
> With or without U, aha,
> I can't play with or without U.
>
> And I try to make **qindar** (**qintar**)
> And you try **qadi** and **qaid**
> And there's **qi**, and there's **qat**
> And you find that you **qanat**.
>
> There's no **qiviut** or **qabala**(**h**),
> No **sheqel** or **mbaqanga**,
> No **qwerty** and there's nothing left sans Us.
>
> And you try to make **faqir**,
> And you try to make **umiaq**,

And there's **qoph**, and there's **tranq**
And you find that you **qanat**.

With or without U
With or without U, oh, oh
I can't play
With or without U.

With or without U
With or without U, oh, ah,
I can't play
With or without U.

Qindar: Albanian currency, equal to one-hundredth of a **lek** (also **qintar**)

Qadi: a judge in Islamic courts (also **kadi**, **cadi**)

Qaid: a Muslim chieftain (also **caid**)

Qi: the central life force in traditional Chinese culture, pronounced "chee" (also **ki**)

Qat: the leaf of a type of shrub, chewed to used in tea as a mild stimulant (also **kat**, **khat**)

Qanat: a gently sloping tunnel used for irrigation

Qiviut: musk-ox wool

Qabala: an occult belief (also **qabalah**, **cabala**, **kabala**)

Sheqel: several ancient Middle Eastern units of weight and money (also **shekel**) (-s, -im)

Mbaqanga: a southern African music style (*from the Zulu umbaqanga, or "steamed cornbread," referring to homemade music that also provides for—and is a metaphorical type of— daily bread*)

Qwerty: used to describe a standard English-language keyboard

Faqir: a Muslim ascetic (also **fakir**)

Umiaq: a wooden, open boat used by Inuit (also **umiac**, **umiack**, **umiak**)

Qoph: a Hebrew letter (also **caph**, **khaf**, **kaph**)

Tranq: a tranquilizer (also **trank**)

Foods That Start with the Letter Q, for 100

In the film *White Men Can't Jump*, Rosie Perez's character shows some of the traits of a competitive Scrabble player in her obsessive studying to prepare for an appearance on *Jeopardy!* She informs her boyfriend that, besides **quince**, she's "got seven more" foods that start with *q* in her arsenal, should the topic come up.

When she appears on *Jeopardy!*, **lo** and behold, one of the categories is "Foods That Start with the Letter Q." We see her answer four questions correctly (or question four answers correctly, it being *Jeopardy!*)—**quail**, **quiche**, **quahog** (a type of clam, also **quohog**), and **quince**.

Here are four more she may have had at the ready:

Quinoa: a starchy grain of the Andes
Quinnat: the chinook, or king salmon
Quenelle: a poached dumpling containing minced fish, chicken, or meat
Quamash: a perennial herb with edible bulbs (*Native Americans introduced roasted quamash bulbs to Lewis and Clark, who thereafter relied heavily upon them.*)

The **carl marl**s while the **jarl** eats **farl**s.

Carl: a peasant or manual laborer (also **carle**)
Marl: to fertilize using a certain type of loose sedimentary soil
Jarl: a Scandinavian chief or nobleman
Farl: a thin triangular bread or cake (also **farle**)

Along the **ria**, a **raia** with a taste for **raki** sells a **rya** to the **raja** and the **rani**.

Ria: long, thin inlet formed by a rising sea level
Raia: a non-Muslim Turk (also **raya**, **rayah**)
Raki: an anise-flavored Turkish liqueur
Rya: a traditional Scandinavian rug
Raja: an Indian monarch (also **rajah**)
Rani: the wife of a rajah (also **ranee**)

The **darb**, an **arb** in the **urb**, wears a **barbut** in the **darbar**.

Darb: someone or something excellent (*popular in the 1920s*)
Arb: an arbitrageur, an investor who sells purchases soon after buying them to capitalize on slightly differing prices
Urb: a city
Barbut: a steel, Greek-style helmet popular in fourteenth- and fifteenth-century Italy
Darbar: a type of Indian court (also **durbar**)

They'll probably **rif** the **reb** because he can't **ref** the **rec** soccer games by the **regs**.

Rif: to lay off from employment (*from "Reduction in Force"*)
Reb: a Southern soldier in the Civil War
Ref: to referee
Rec: recreation
Reg: regulation

The **lar gars** the **sowar** to hurl the **bola** at the **boyar.**

Lar: a spirit of the ancient Roman household
Gar: to force or compel
Sowar: a horseback soldier in India
Bola: a weapon of weighted balls connected by a cord thrown to catch cattle (*connected to the idea of the bolo tie*)
Boyar: a member of the former Russian aristocracy

No **sal sall** be added to the **salep** or the **saloop.**

Sal: salt
Sall: shall (**Sall** *can't be conjugated—this is its only form.*)
Salep: a flour ground from orchid tubers and used in food and medicine
Saloop: a hot tea of aromatic herbs

The **puss** will **buss** the **joss**, then **doss** in a **foss.**

Puss: a cat
Buss: to kiss
Joss: a Chinese shrine or idol
Doss: to sleep, particularly in a convenient, crude place
Foss: a moat or ditch (also **fosse**)

"S-ential"

Everyone knows those four Ss are a huge help for tacking on the ends of words, but they also help start words. The most Scrabble words by far start with *s* (about 20,000). Surprisingly, the second and third most common letters to start Scrabble words with are *c* (about 16,000) and *p* (about 15,000). Less surprising, the least numerous first letters are *x* (152), *y* (588), *z* (601), and *q* (850).

When I scry and espy my tyned sib, I lose my sel and sab.

Scry: to look into a crystal ball for answers
Espy: to catch sight of
Tyne: to perish, to lose (*as in "to become lost"*) (also **tine**)
Sib: a sibling
Sel: self
Sab: to sob

The sei is such a seg she even keeps her sox separated.

Sei: a small baleen whale
Seg: a racial segregationist
Sox: socks, a plural of sock

The sri in the suq accepts sers of sens, saus, sous or soms.

Sri: an Indian title of respect akin to *Mr.*
Suq: a large marketplace (also **suk, souk**)
Ser: a former unit of volume in India equal to a liter
Sen: a monetary unit of Japan equal to one-hundredth of a yen
Sau: a monetary unit of Vietnam equal to one-hundredth of a dong (also **xu**)
Sou: a former French coin (*Today, in French* sou *refers to any coin of little worth, and one can say "sans le sou," as in, "I'm broke."*)
Som: a monetary unit of several Central Asian countries

First they joist the kist. Neist they'll hist the cist.

Joist: to support from beneath with parallel horizontal wooden or steal beams
Kist: a chest or coffin
Neist: next
Hist: to hoist
Cist: a prehistoric tomb of stone or hollowed wood

The tui, the tit, and the mut tut a "tsk" at the teg on the tor.

Tui: a common bird of New Zealand also known as the honeyeater
Tit: a small bird also known as the titmouse or chickadee
Mut: a mutt
Tut: to make a sound of disapproval or impatience
Tsk: an expression of disapproval (also **tsktsk**)
Teg: a sheep before it is shorn (also **tegg**)
Tor: rocky hill or peak

"This is some teuch, teugh, tough tuff."

Teuch: tough (also **teugh**)
Tuff: rock made of consolidated volcanic ash

Softly, softly played the potto—but not tanto—on the koto during the tutti in the lento.

Potto: a small, nocturnal lemur of tropical Africa also known as the softly-softly
Tanto: too much—used as a musical direction, generally with a negative connotation
Koto: a traditional Japanese stringed musical instrument
Tutti: a passage of music played by all performers
Lento: a slow movement in a musical composition

The tahr in the talar stotts at the sett by the yett.

Tahr: an Asian goatlike mammal
Talar: a long cloak
Stott: to pronk, to leap upward with arched back (*used of an animal*) (also **stot**)
Sett: a badger's burrow
Yett: an iron gate for a doorway, typically found in castles and tower houses in Scotland

The **tyee**, a **tyro**, **tost** the **rotte** into the **mott**.

Tyee: the king salmon, also known as the chinook or quinnat
Tyro: a novice
Tost: a past tense of toss
Rotte: a stringed instrument in sixth-century Germany
Mott: a small cluster of trees, typically on a prairie (also **motte**)

The **uta** on the **ute** played an **ut** on his **uke**.

Uta: the side-blotched lizard
Ute: a utility vehicle
Ut: the note "do" in the French solmization system
Uke: ukulele

On their **zebec**, the **zebu** and the **kudu tabu** talk of the **habu**, **kagu**, and **kombu**. And no **gnu**, neither!

Zebec: a small, three-masted Mediterranean sailing vessel (also **xebec**)
Zebu: a type of Asiatic cattle
Kudu: a large striped antelope native to Africa (also **koodoo**)
Tabu: to refrain from doing or mentioning (also **taboo**) (-ed, -ing, -s)
Habu: any of certain poisonous snakes in Japan
Kagu: a nearly flightless, endangered white bird of New Caledonia
Kombu: kelp used as soup seasoning in Japanese cooking
Gnu: a wildebeest

The **umbo** protects the **ululant ulan's ulna**.

Umbo: the central rounded piece at the center of a shield, also known as a shield-boss
Ululant: screaming
Ulan: a member of the Polish light cavalry (also **uhlan**)

Ulna: a long bone of the forearm

The **hun**, a **mun** dressed in **dun**, broke the **unco's unci** and **nam** his **jun**.

Hun: a barbarous, brutal person
Mun: a fellow
Dun: of a brownish gray color
Unco: a stranger or an unusual person (*from uncouth*)
Unci: plural of **uncus:** any hook-shaped anatomical part, often the curved anterior of the parahippocampal gyrus
Nam: past tense of **nim:** to steal
Jun: a coin used in North Korea (pl. **jun**)

The **lulu** in the **iglu** cuts her **sulu** with an **ulu**.

Lulu: something remarkable, often referring to a woman
Iglu: igloo
Sulu: a Fijian skirt worn by men and women
Ulu: an Inuit knife

The **supe**, a **yup** with an **updo**, **sups upo scup** beneath an **upas**. **Upby**, a **fou ouph** with a **pouf urps**.

Supe: a minor actor without a speaking part, a supernumerary
Yup: a yuppie

Updo: any hair style whereby the hair is arranged—such as in a beehive or ponytail—rather than letting it fall freely
Sup: to eat dinner
Upo: upon
Scup: the common porgy fish
Upas: an Asian tree famous for its poisonous sap
Upby: farther along ahead at a specific place (also **upbye**)
Fou: drunk
Ouph: an elf, sprite, or similar small, mischievous creature (also **ouphe**)
Pouf: a hairstyle involving a bump or large elevated wave of hair toward the front of the top of the head (also **pouff**)
Urp: to vomit

The **wud fud** wins a **kudo** for his **udo pud.**

Wud: crazy
Fud: a fuddy-duddy, one who is old-fashioned and opposed to excitement
Kudo: praise, a compliment
Udo: an east-Asian herb used in cooking, such as miso soup
Pud: pudding

"**Brava, bobby,** for bagging the **bravo** who stole the **avo** yesterday **arvo.**"
"Oh, I only yelled '**Avast!**' It was nothing **ava! Ave!**"

Brava: an exclamation of applause
Bobby: a police officer (chiefly British)
Bravo: a professional killer (pl. -vos or -voes or -vi)
Avo: a unit of currency in Macao worth one-hundredth of a pataca
Arvo: afternoon
Avast: an exclamation used to command one to stop
Ava: at all
Ave: a poetic salutation of greeting or parting (as in "Ave Maria" or "Hail Mary")

In the **vid**, the **dev** with the deep **vox revs** the **vis** of the **vac** with **vim** so he can **veg** in the **lav** again.

Vid: a video
Dev: a Hindu god (also **deva**)
Vox: voice
Rev: to quickly accelerate
Vis: force or strength (pl. **vires**)
Vac: a vacuum cleaner
Vim: enthusiasm
Veg: to be idle
Lav: a bathroom

The **vireo** and **veery** enjoy **venery** in the **vert veld**, and the **avadavant** in the **vanda** like **banda**. **Viva! Vive!**

Vireo: a small bird
Veery: a songbird
Venery: sexual intercourse
Vert: a heraldic shade of green
Veld: grassland of southern Africa (also **veldt**)
Avadavant: a small songbird
Vanda: a tropical orchard
Banda: a traditional, bass-heavy Mexican dance music
Viva: a shout of encouragement or exultation (also **vive**)

Vum! says the **vrow** when she stubs her toe in the **vug** by the **voe**.

Vum: an exclamation of surprise
Vrow: a woman (also **vrouw**) (*from the same Dutch word meaning "woman" or "wife"*)
Vug: a small cavity in a rock, often lined with crystals (also **vugg**, **vugh**)
Voe: a small bay or inlet

The **vizir** likes diverse **vivers** with his **vichy** and **vino**.

Vizir: a minister or high official in a Muslim government (also **vizier**)
Vivers: (n./pl.) food, provisions
Vichy: mineral water from Vichy, France, or a replica thereof
Vino: wine

In the **weald**, the **wakanda** will protect your **wikiup**, but **wite** the **windigo** if a **williwaw wigwag**s your **wigwam**.

Weald: a wooded area, or an open field
Wakanda: the central animating spirit in Sioux spirituality
Wikiup: a domed American Indian hut (also **wigwam, wickiup**)
Wite: to blame (also **wyte**)
Windigo: an evil spirit in Algonquian mythology that overtakes a person with cannibalistic urges (also **wendigo**)
Williwaw: a violent, cold wind blowing down from a mountain (also **willyway** and **williwau**)
Wigwag: to move to and fro
Wigwam: a domed American Indian hut (also **wickiup**)

Phew. Every day I **tew** to **hew** the **yew**. Let me **shew** you my **thew**. You'll make a **whew**.

Phew: an expression of relief
Tew: to work hard
Hew: to cleave with an axe
Yew: several types of large, poisonous evergreen trees or shrubs that can live for thousands of years
Shew: to show
Thew: musculature (adj. **thewy**)
Whew: a sound made to illustrate amazement or relief

Once in a while, the **wittol wiss**es a **widdy** will take his **wifey awa**.

Wittol: a cuckold who permits or condones his wife's infidelity

Wiss: to wish
Widdy: a noose (also **widdie**)
Wifey: a wife
Awa: away

The **wivern** in the **welkin waff**s at the **raff**.

Wivern: a legendary dragon-headed lizard with a barbed tail (also
wyvern)
Welkin: the celestial sphere, the vaulted sky
Waff: to wave
Raff: riffraff

Wisha! That **wany wavelet**'s a **waly**!

Wisha: an expression of surprise
Wany: visibly decreasing in size (also **waney**)
Wavelet: a small wave
Waly: something pleasing, especially to the eye (also **wally**)

I'm a **wee, twee tween**.
I'm **weer**, you **weet**.
I'm **weest**, you **wist**.

Wee: very little
Twee: affectedly or excessively cute
Tween: a child after mid-childhood but before puberty, generally
between eight and twelve years old
Weer: even littler
Weet: to know, to wit
Weest: the littlest of a group
Wist: to know (past tense: **wis**) (**Wis** *and* **wist** *are the only forms
of this verb.*)

When I **wale** you **weel** you'll **wark** and **wawl** with the **weal**s
and **whelk**s.

Wale: to injure, to create welts on the skin

Weel: well
Wark: to feel pain, to ache
Wawl: to cry like a cat (also **waul**)
Weal: a welt
Whelk: a pustule, a pimple

The **wiggy wack** wearing one **welly** awaits the **weka** in the **wahoo**.

Wiggy: insane
Wack: very bad, or a zany person
Welly: a rainboot (also **wellie**) *(named after Arthur Wellesley, first Duke of Wellington, whose wearing of them popularized them among the British aristocracy in the early nineteenth century)*
Weka: a flightless bird of New Zealand also called the woodhen
Wahoo: a flowering American shrub with heart-shaped poisonous berries

Ywis, I **wiss** I **wis wha** the **wud wiz** was.

Ywis: absolutely (also **iwis**)
Wiss: to wish

Wis: knew (past tense of **wist:** to know, to be aware of)
Wha: who
Wud: crazy
Wiz: wizard

The **prex** acts more like a **rex**: He likes to down **dex**, **rax** his rule, and eschews **lex** or **doxy**.

Prex: a president, usually of a college (also **prexy**)
Rex: a king (pl. **reges**); or a species of cat with a single layer of fine hair, also known as the Cornish Rex (pl. **rexes**)
Dex: a sulfate used as a stimulant (**dexy** and **dexie:** a tablet thereof)
Rax: to stretch or reach out
Lex: law (pl. **leges**)
Doxy: accepted ideas or doctrine

The **nix** on the **kex** was **vext** by the **nixy** she'd sent to the **pixy** on the **falx**.

Nix: a water sprite in German folklore (pl. **nixes**, **nixe**, a female is a **nixie**), or to veto
Kex: any of several types of hollow-stalked plants
Vext: irritated, annoyed (a past tense of **vex**)
Nixy: mail that is undeliverable
Pixy: a mythical, miniature playful sprite

X Marks the Spot

One letter a player should *always* be happy to see is the *x*, with its high value and easy usability in two-letter words (**ax**, **ex**, **xi**, **ox**, **xu**). With all these two-letter combos, it's generally best (and easiest) to play the *x* for big points by using it both horizontally and vertically at once.

Falx: any sickle-shaped structure, generally used of blades or anatomical parts (pl. **falces**)

Until the **xyst** is **fixt**, the **eaux** spoils the **jeux**.

Xyst: the covered portico of a Greek gymnasium used in inclem-
ent weather (also **xystus**)
Fixt: a past tense of *fix*
Eaux: waters (pl. of **eau:** water)
Jeux: games (pl. of **jeu:** game)

The **ixodid**—or is it a **cimex**?—is **dexter** of my **oxter**.

Ixodid: a tick
Cimex: a bedbug
Dexter: situated on the right (as opposed to **sinister**, on the left)
Oxter: the armpit

The **oxes** want their drinks to make a **fiz**, but since they don't
have **gox**, they **lox** their soda so it's **oxo**.

Oxes: plural of **ox:** oaf (*as opposed to* **oxen**, *which is the plural of the
animal*)
Fiz: a sound similar to that of a carbonated beverage
Gox: gaseous oxygen
Lox: to supply with liquid oxygen
Oxo: containing oxygen (also **oxy**)

In the **ley**, the **gey fey dey fleys** the **bey's quey**.

Ley: a meadow (also **lea**)
Gey: very
Fey: insane
Dey: the title given to rulers of some Ottoman Empire lands
Fley: to scare
Bey: an Ottoman Empire provincial governor
Quey: a heifer

... and Sometimes Y

Have a rack with no vowels except a Y or two? **Oy**! But don't cry. Though the *y* can be a trying letter to play, **ay** (a vote yes, also **aye**), **ya** (you), **by**, **my**, **yo**, and **oy** give **ye** (you) some options. There are also some words that use only *ys* as vowels.

Down the **wynd** and past the **wych**, the **sylph** with **syph** wonders the **whys** of the world.

Wynd: an alleyway
Wych: a type of European elm also known as the Scots elm
Sylph: a slender girl or young woman who moves gracefully
Syph: syphilis (-s)
Why: the reason for

The **pyknic's tyke rykes** out into the **syke** with his **fyke**.

Pyknic: a person with a rotund or stocky build
Tyke: a toddler
Ryke: to reach
Syke: a small stream
Fyke: a fishing net

The **sayyid payed** many **tyiyn** and moved **inby** to see the **syzygy** painted on the **skyey** ceiling.

Sayyid: the title *lord* or *sir* used for a Muslim man (also **sayid**)
Payed: an alternate spelling of **paid**
Tyiyn: a monetary unit of Kyrgyzstan worth one-hundredth of a **som**
Inby: into a house or room
Syzygy: an alignment of three celestial bodies, as in the sun, moon, and earth during an eclipse
Skyey: sky-like

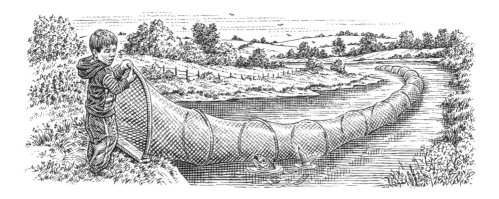

The **yeld yaud** was **yald**.

Yeld: a mature female not giving milk
Yaud: a mare of old age
Yald: robust, lively (also **yauld**)

Our **biz** is the best at cleaning the **zin** and **za** from your **tux**.

Biz: business
Zin: Zinfandel wine
Za: pizza
Tux: a tuxedo

Z

The **zoril** holds a **zori** and a **zill**.

Zoril: a small African weasel (also **zorilla**, **zorrille**, **zorillo**)
Zori: a flat, thonged Japanese sandal
Zill: a finger cymbal

The **zek** gets a **zax** and an **adz**, but not a **zep**.

Zek: an inmate, particularly of a Soviet labor camp
Zax: a tool used in applying slate to a roof
Adz: to carve wood with an adz (a curved blade attached to a
handle) (also **adze**)

Zep: a particular type of hoagie sandwich from eastern Pennsylvania

In the movie, the nasty **nazi** steals a **yagi** to control the **azo azon** from the **ghazi.**

Nazi: a racist fascist, or increasingly any dictatorial and intolerant person
Yagi: a type of antenna useful with amateur radio enthusiasts

Jazzy Multi-Z Words You'll Probably Never Use

Fezzed, Fezzy: adjectives related to **fez** (a brimless hat worn by men in Turkey)
Frizz: to form into small, tight curls
Hazzan: a cantor (pl. **hazzanim**)
Huzza: to cheer (**huzzah**, **huzzas**)
Izzard: the letter *z*
Jazzbo: a devotee of jazz
Mezuzah: a small Judaic scroll (**mezuza**)
Mizzen: a type of sail
Mizzle: to rain in fine droplets (**mizzly**)
Muzzy: confused
Nuzzle: to push with the nose
Pizzle: the penis of an animal (*Primarily in Australia and New Zealand, though it also crops up in James Joyce's Ulysses. Also occasionally found in the combination "bull pizzle," denoting a whip made from a bull's penis, as in Samuel Beckett's radio play* Rough for Radio II.)
Zugzwang: a move in a game—generally chess—that a player is compelled to make and that significantly worsens the player's position (*from the German meaning "compulsion to move"*) (*I cannot think of such an instance occurring in Scrabble, as players always have the option of passing*)
Zuz: an ancient Hebrew coin (pl. **zuzim**)
Zzz: used to express being asleep

Azo: containing nitrogen
Azon: a guided aerial bomb used by the Allies in World War II
(*from AZimuth ONly*)
Ghazi: a Muslim war hero (*from the Ghazwa battles led by Muhammed*)

> The **zerk** is **oozy**, not **sizy**.

Zerk: a grease fitting, also known as a grease nipple
Oozy: containing or resembling soft mud or slime
Sizy: thick and sticky

MISCELLANEOUS

> "**Yah**! I feel sick. I think I'm going **ralph vomito** out my **os**."
> "Don't! If you **bevomit** yourself with **vomitus**, I might **upchuck**."
> "Well if you **urp**, I could **keck** a whole lot of **yech**."
> "**Ick**! Watching **emesis** always makes me **regorge**!"
> "**Oops**, I **woops**ed!"
> "**Ugh**, you **spewers** are **ugsome**."

Yah: an exclamation of disgust
Ralph: to vomit
Vomito: the black vomit associated with yellow fever
Os: an orifice
Bevomit: to vomit all over oneself
Vomitus: vomit
Upchuck: to vomit
Urp: to vomit
Keck: to retch
Yech: something gross (also **yecch**, **yechy**, **yuch**, and **yucch**)
Ick: an expression of disgust
Emesis: the act of vomiting (**emetic:** a substance that is ingested to induce emesis)
Regorge: to vomit
Oops: an expression of mild apology, surprise, or dismay

Woops: to vomit
Ugh: used to suggest a cough or grunt
Spewer: one who vomits
Ugsome: gross

The **guv**'s **luv** is a **fauve** who keeps her **kuvasz** in the **lav.**

Guv: a governor
Luv: a sweetheart
Fauve: a fauvist
Kuvasz: a large breed of dog with a white coat (also **kuvaszo**)
Lav: a bathroom

The **jato** felt more like a **rato** to the **dato** in the **rabato.**

Jato: a jet-assisted takeoff (*an example of an acronym turned playable word*)
Rato: a rocket-assisted takeoff (*another example of an acronym turned playable word*)
Dato: a tribal chief in the Philippines (also **datto**)
Rabato: a type of collar with a laced edge

A **gaga dodo** in a **bubu**, a **coocoo kaka** in a **mumu**, and a **chichi nana** in a **tutu** go to the **dada gogo.**

Gaga: insane
Dodo: a large extinct bird incapable of flight
Bubu: a large, flowing garment (also **boubou**)
Coocoo: lunatic
Kaka: a parrot native to New Zealand
Mumu: a long, loose-fitting dress (also **muumuu**)
Chichi: affectedly stylish
Nana: a grandmother
Tutu: a short skirt worn by ballerinas
Dada: an artistic movement interested in subverting rationality
Gogo: a disco party

The **mama ouistiti** says to the **papa dikdik**, "If you need to **weewee** or make a **doodoo** or **caca**, do it by the **kaki** or the **titi** outside the **haha**."

Mama: a mother
Ouistiti: a monkey native to South America
Papa: a father
Dikdik: a small antelope
Weewee: to urinate
Doodoo: fecal matter
Caca: fecal matter
Kaki: a Japanese persimmon tree
Titit: a type of evergreen shrub
Haha: a sunken fence, used to separate property without blighting the landscape

If you like this book, **bakshish** the bookseller or give a **cumshaw** to the librarian who showed it to you.

Bakshish: to give a tip (**baksheesh**)
Cumshaw: a gift (*usually a tip for service*)

SOURCES

Burkeman, Oliver. "Spellbound." Retrieved from www.guardian. co.uk/lifeandstyle/2008/jun/28/healthandwellbeing. familyandrelationships.

Fatsis, Stefan. *Word Freak: Heartbreak, Triumph, Genius, and Obsession in the World of Competitive Scrabble Players.* Boston: Houghton Mifflin, 2001.

Lacey, Marc. " 'Haboobs' Stir Critics in Arizona." Retrieved from www.nytimes.com/2011/07/22/us/22haboob.html.

McCarthy, Paul. *Letterati: An Unauthorized Look at Scrabble and the People Who Play It.* Toronto: ECW Press, 2008.

Morris, Chris. "Now Legal in Scrabble: Thang, Blingy and Grrl." Retrieved from www.cnbc.com/id/42991790/ Now_Legal_in_Scrabble_Thang_Blingy_and_Grrl).

North American Scrabble Players Association (NASPA). [Source for records.] Retrieved from www.scrabbleplayers.org/w/Records.

Seattle Scrabble Club. [Source for some lists.] Retrieved from www.seattlescrabble.org.

Smith, Keith W. *Total Scrabble: The (Un)Official Scrabble Record Book,* January 2009 Update. Retrieved from http://cross-tables.com/ download/totalscrabble.pdf.

Spahn, Mark. [Probabilities of various letter combina- tions.] Retrieved from www.mathkb.com/Uwe/Forum.aspx/ recreational/2449/Scrabble-probabilities.

Wallace, Robert. "A Man Makes a Best-Selling Game—Scrabble—and Achieves His Ambition (Spelled Out Above)." *Life,* Vol. 35, No. 24. Dec. 14, 1953.

Wapnick, Joel. *How to Play Scrabble Like a Champion.* New York: Puzzlewright Press, 2010.

DICTIONARIES

Official Scrabble Players Dictionary, Fourth Edition (OSPD). This is
the current edition, published in 2005. Where older editions are
mentioned, they refer to
OSPD1, the *Official Scrabble Players Dictionary, First Edition.* 1978.
OSPD2, the *Official Scrabble Players Dictionary, Second Edition.* 1993.
OSPD3, the *Official Scrabble Players Dictionary, Third Edition.* 1996.

Merriam-Webster's Collegiate Dictionary, Eleventh Edition, 2003.
(MWCD11).

The Oxford English Dictionary (OED), 1971 edition.

Official Tournament and Club Word List, Second Edition. (OWL or
OWL2). Merriam-Webster, 2006.